To

Have

AND

To

Hold

The riage

D1372220

Val Farmer, Ph.D.

JV Publishing, LLC
Casselton, North Dakota

Published by
JV Publishing, LLC
P.O. Box 886
Casselton, North Dakota
58012

Library of Congress Control Number: 2006933279

Farmer, Val 1940 -
    To Have and To Hold

ISBN: 0-9787561-0-X
    1. Marriage

Cover Design by flintcommunications, Fargo, ND

Interior book design by Katy Oliver
Oliver Press, Pelican Rapids, MN

Printed in the United States of America

Other Books by Val Farmer

Honey, I Shrunk The Farm

Making The Good Life Better

To The Reader

Throughout my career as a psychologist and columnist, I have strongly believed that a loving marriage is essential to happiness. I believe that marriage is a part of God's plan for the human family in this mortal existence. The urge to bond with a lifetime companion is a profound and compelling part of human experience. In the intimacy of marriage, we experience joy, support, companionship, passion and purpose. But it can also be a source of profound pain, sorrow, discouragement and despair.

Marriage stretches us. If we can apply the principles of love, kindness and reconciliation under the duress of conflict and differences with an intimate partner we can apply them anywhere. It is the crucible in which we gradually shed ourselves of selfishness and baser impulses and learn to freely give love and service to others.

I have experienced joy and growth in my association with my wife, Darlene. Many of my insights into marriage have come in the context of living what is now a 40 year marriage.

My life has also been enriched by flesh and blood examples of couples who have come to me for counsel. Distilled into this book are thoughts and ideas of things I have learned as I have counseled them in their struggles and heartaches.

I value the knowledge of others, - psychologists, sociologists, researchers, therapists, religious leaders and authors of inspirational literature. You will see throughout this book a broad range of people who have contributed to the understanding of what it takes to have a good marriage.

There are many ways to improve an already good marriage. Tried and tested ideas presented in this book can enrich your marriage and make it even better. Other chapters are filled with information and detail in addressing many problems that may occur in marriage. Don't be overwhelmed by the possibilities. Many of these problems may never be experienced in your marriage. But if they are, you will have a starting place to turn to for sound advice and counsel.

The value of our individual contributions to society will eventually fade. Time will see to that. But the legacy of a strong marriage where love and values are passed from generation to generation and will never fade. It's worth the effort of a lifetime.

"Do you believe in marriage? Val Farmer does, and more than just believe in it, he understands how the marriage relationship works and what can make it better. His book, based on a lifetime of personal experience and the best scholarly research, is filled with sound theory and practical, usable ideas. It is the best scientific and human wisdom made available to pastors, counselors — to all of us. Val Farmer knows what he's talking about. He'll keep you believing in marriage, too!"

- Reverend Doctor Peter L. Schmidt, Senior Pastor, Faith Lutheran Church, West Fargo, ND

Acknowledgments

To Julie Burgum: Thank you for providing the inspiration and encouragement to bring this book out to the public.

To Katy Oliver: Thank you for your skill and professional expertise in making this book highly readable and pleasant to the eye.

To my wife Darlene: Thank you for your unerring sense of judgment and for not letting me get by without giving my best.

To Dixie Davis of the Preston Connection: Thank you for lifting my load, for laying the groundwork and for your steadfast efforts of getting this material ready over the years on a weekly basis.

To Trista and Darin Andersen: Thank you for your support and for your painstaking editing. I truly appreciate the second and third mile you have gone for me throughout the years.

To the researchers who I've interviewed: Thank you for graciously sharing your knowledge on personal relationships.

To couples who I've seen in counseling: Thank you for your trust. Your problems and your lives make it all real and keep me in touch with the human condition.

Dedication

Darlene, heaven will not be heaven to me
if I do not meet you there.

Table of Contents

Part I: A Great Beginning

I will always cherish the initial
misconceptions I had about you.
- Unknown

ON BECOMING A COUPLE
CHAPTER ONE

Remember the awe and admiration that first attracted you? You wanted someone special. You experienced the exhilaration and wonder of falling in love, the excitement of sexual attraction, the easy conversations, the soul sharing, the adventures and the gifts of love.

Your blind idealization of each other will sustain you when you become acquainted with the reality of your loved one's weaknesses and imperfections. Keep alive the image of who you once were and how it all began. Your bright memories of radiant love will cushion your disappointment and anger when your partner falls short. You need double vision. One vision sees and remembers the reservoir of love and goodness that was there from the start. The other vision sees your partner in cold reality. Be willing to confront truth, work for change and give honest feedback so that your relationship can grow and improve.

Leave your parents behind and together form a new identity - a marriage. Shift the "I" of your individuality over to the "we" of marriage. Put a "we" around your marriage and protect it as a separate entity. You are individuals within a marriage, not two separate people who live side-by-side and share common interests.

Some of your early clashes will occur as you both learn to sacrifice your individual wants and desires and give attention and nurturing to the marriage. What might be best for you might not be best for the marriage. It will take a conscious effort to love, show empathy, share and yield to mutual interests.

The other side of the coin is to allow for and accept differences, privacy and autonomy. As you change and grow, you'll need to fine tune your marriage to adjust to each other's individual changing priorities.

Learn about and come to depend on each other's habits of thought, expression and basic assumptions. Each of you will become increasingly accurate in anticipating and correctly identifying your partner's feelings and attitudes.

Personal identity is strengthened when you share common meanings, perceptions and understandings. More importantly, your own view of yourself will depend to some measure on how your spouse sees and responds to you. Your mate also depends on you for that personal feedback.

You use each other to remember past events. Your partner doesn't have to remember a particular event or detail because he or she knows you will remember it - and vice versa. The more interdependent you become, the more your memories are held jointly. To lose your partner is to lose memory - to lose a part of yourself.

Create a safe haven for the expression of difference, anger and conflict. How you handle conflict is crucial to the satisfaction you'll have in your marriage. Two strong people with definite ideas, expectations and histories are going to collide. Establish a safety zone for tolerating the expression of strong emotion without letting it threaten your commitment to the marriage.

Don't withdraw and nurse grudges. Be willing to talk through your difficulties. Don't explode in anger and say harsh and cruel things that wound the soul. Learn to be accepting and easy going. Disengage if emotions are too high and then come back to the issue within a mutually agreed time frame.

Even at the height of your dismay and emotional storms, modulate your anger and behavior so you don't endanger your connection. Be the first to reach out with overtures of love and reconciliation.

Make the effort to build your marriage by consistent, loving actions. Be willing to put the well-being and happiness of your partner ahead of your own self-interest. The strength of your bond depends on the amount of effort put into the marriage.

The value of a relationship grows with time. As a couple, you accumulate a store of shared experiences that give your life together meaning.

The length of the marriage is a factor. Emotional investment isn't just about the amount of time you spend together but also about the quality of your shared experiences. Your bond is deepened by shared memories and activities. Marriage is still about fun and doing things together. It is about sharing deep emotional experiences, personal thoughts, feelings, fantasies, hopes and dreams.

Invest in each other. Another type of sharing is the gift of freedom, support and acceptance you give one another in helping each other grow and develop along unique paths. Support and encourage your partner's efforts at becoming his or her best self. Invest your time, interest and attention in helping your partner become the good and desirable person he or she wants to be.

Your investment is an investment in each other - a history of the many reciprocal acts of love and personal sacrifice for the other's well-being. As time passes, both of you have a stake in the talents and qualities of each other.

TWELVE WAYS TO HAVE AN EXCELLENT MARRIAGE
CHAPTER TWO

Here are twelve suggestions on how to work toward having an excellent marriage. Great marriages make for very happy lives. Mediocre marriages may or may not contribute much to personal happiness. Bad marriages make for unhappy lives. With extra work and attention, many couples can transform their marriages from mediocre to wonderful.

To help bad marriages become good and then become wonderful may take counseling or extra focus on eliminating destructive behavior from the relationship. A list of ten "don'ts" is included in chapter six, "Why Marriages Fall Apart."

1. Be loyal. In the ups and downs of life, the only thing you have to fall back on is your character and honor in keeping the promises you made to each other at the time of marriage. There will be times of unhappiness and vulnerability.

Remember your wedding vows and the expectations of your friends, family and community. Do all that is required of you to honor your marriage. Protect your relationship from outside influences and alternatives. Commitment is the bedrock that holds couples together when other forces pull them apart.

This expectation of faithfulness continues during adversity, illness, disability, aging and other trials of life. Honor your commitment even when it calls for personal hardship and sacrifice.

Trust is built on honesty and fidelity. Keep confidential your intimate conversations. Protect your marriage by respecting boundaries of physical and emotional intimacy that should never be crossed in opposite sex friendships. Don't disparage your partner in private or in public.

Keep your partner's confidences. There are important needs for sexual and emotional intimacy that can only be satisfied in the marriage and *nowhere* else. You have a private world that takes precedence over all other relationships. Your private world consists of goals, personal struggles, secret thoughts, memories and joys that belong and are known only to the two of you.

2. Show love through actions on a daily basis. Serving one another, loving and giving, sacrificing for the other's well being, and consistently putting one's partner ahead of oneself is important. How you treat one another should be an example of your love. Your actions are the crucible for love and happiness.

Small changes in your behavior may be the trigger that will make a difference - not only to your partner but also to your own feelings of love, attraction and satisfaction. Add small acts of kindness and concern to your relationship while subtracting acts of thoughtlessness, meanness or neglect. You don't have control over your partner's behavior but you do have control over your own.

The lubricant of love consists of daily acts of consideration, kindness, courtesy, and attention. One put-down will erase many hours of kindness shown to a partner.

Love loosens the bands of selfishness. By experimenting with love, you will find that the love you freely give comes back to you.

Anticipate and meet your spouse's emotional needs through daily acts of love and consideration. Be there for each other in times of joy and times of sorrow or threat. Sacrifice for his or her grow..., wishes and even whims. Encourage and support each other's goa.. he or she pursues individual gifts and talents.

Have a willing attitude about pleasing your partner and responding to requests and concerns. Ease one another's burdens. Freely give your love, even when it is difficult or inconvenient.

3. Express affection, admiration, appreciation and fondness. Express appreciation and admiration for those wonderful qualities that attracted you in the first place. Appreciate the new qualities that you discover as you live your lives together.

Expressions of love and appreciation for special qualities or efforts mean a lot. It goes beyond words to loving touches, embraces and holding. It includes physical proximity, special looks and loving eye contact.

After you've been apart, greet your loved one with delight and enthusiasm. Let your partner know with your eyes, smile and a loving embrace that you are happy to be back in his or her presence. As you part, acknowledge your importance and love for each other.

Reaffirm your love and connection as a couple. Develop your own intimate rituals and language of love. Don't lose touch with each other in the midst of busy lives and demands. Your lives need to be integrated and coordinated.

4. Share your lives through emotional intimacy. Create and share a private world where you confide deeply about life, joys, fears, hurts, frustrations and challenges. Talk often and openly about feelings and wonderment. Stay in touch with the details of each other's emotional lives.

Use each other as sounding boards for talking a problem out loud, working through issues and gaining a valued perspective. Turn to each other for advice and comfort. Be a good listener. Show empathy, interest and concern.

5. Enjoy each other's companionship. Spend time together and take pleasure in each other's companionship. Laugh and play together. Enjoy each other's sense of humor. Find common interests. Make memories. Have adventures together. Take special vacations. Be playful. Relax and unwind together. Enjoy humor together. Be easy to be around. Take time for leisure and light-hearted fun. Take time for yourselves as a couple and nourish your marriage.

6. Keep romance alive. The euphoric "falling in love"

experience leads to trust and commitment to each other in an exclusive and permanent bond. Without this base of "chemistry" and powerful attraction, marriage becomes a lot harder.

Make your marriage full of special surprises. Surprise your spouse with a vacation, a special date night, flowers, candy, special gifts or whatever excites him or her. Take the time to really know each other so your surprises have meaning. Marriage needs regular sexual fulfillment. Set the stage so the spark of passion stays alive.

Celebrate your love by honoring birthdays, anniversaries, holidays, and special occasions with gusto and verve. Plan thoughtful, romantic surprises in which you show your loved one that you cherish him or her. Be affectionate. Give plenty of hugs, compliments, kisses, loving touches and caresses and tender expressions of endearment.

Let your daily acts of unselfish love for your partner be the context for your sexual relationships. Within the limits of your partner's satisfaction, enjoy the abandonment and pleasure of a dynamic sexual relationship. Make your sexual interactions a lifelong source of mutual enjoyment and love.

7. Operate as a team. Dream together and build a future together. Accept each other's influence and ideas. Work out differences with respect, patience, flexibility and a genuine spirit of learning. Focus on being kind and not on being right. Even if you disagree, be soft in the way you talk to each other.

Coordinate schedules and activities together. Plan and make decisions together. Parent as a team. Share the work of the home and family fairly and equitably. You may have different roles but you are obligated to help each other as equal and cooperative partners. Support both your own family commitments and the extended family obligations as a team. Worship together and share your spiritual journey.

Manage money as a team. Share your resources. Plan your finances and honor your budgetary agreements. Money matters will test your unselfishness and your ability to negotiate and unify around common goals.

8. Manage your personal stress. Don't bring anger, frustration and hurt from work or other situations into your home and unfairly take it out on those you love. Your home and marriage should be a haven and a place of peace.

Be the first to love when love seems lacking. Make your love dependable and as independent as possible from your partner's mood and behavior.

Take care of yourself through rest, leisure, exercise and pleasant personal diversions. This will allow you to give energy to the marriage instead of being a source of strain and worry. Support your spouse's need for leisure, relaxation and personal renewal.

9. Be accepting of differences. Accept your partner's feelings, differences and idiosyncrasies. Show patience and tolerance with each other's weaknesses and imperfections that are not vital to the marriage.

It's not the differences between partners that cause problems but how the differences are handled when they arise. It's not differences and disagreements that cause difficulties. It is the lack of understanding and acceptance of differences. Good listening is a key. A partner is a friend and an equal, not a judge or a counselor. Accept each other as you are.

Love your partner in spite of differences in value judgments or aspects of personality that will never change. Nobody is perfect. Enjoy his or her positive qualities and overlook or put up with the negative.

As much as humanly possible, eliminate harshness, criticism, angry outbursts, disrespectful judgments, blame, contempt, defensiveness, verbal attacks, put-downs and misguided expectations. Your loved one needs to know that he or she has a true friend and is safe with you. Your home should be a haven, not a battleground.

Moderate your reactions to a partner's destructive acts and inhibit your impulse to retaliate or react in kind. In the interest of the relationship, there are times when unfairness and hurt needs to be absorbed. Be willing to de-escalate and dampen down an argument rather than to provocatively up the ante. Minimize conflict and hostility.

Courteous, polite, respectful conversation will underscore your love. Keep in mind that your partner has a unique and valid perspective on life. His or her feelings or opinions have value. They need to be understood and respected. Be open to influence. Don't be so "right" that your loved one has to fight to be heard. How you feel about each other after differences have been aired is more important than what was solved.

10. Develop skills for resolving conflict. A couple who can solve problems together can correct their relationship and keep it on course. Be willing to confront problems, work through differences, take constructive action and persevere when satisfaction wanes or when the relationship is threatened or harmed.

You demonstrate this willingness to confront when you try to improve conditions by talking problems over, seeking help, or by changing behavior to solve a problem. You take seriously your partner's concerns and are willing to work for mutually acceptable solutions.

The ability to communicate effectively and solve problems keeps hope alive. Both partners have faith that conditions can be improved by their ability to exert their personal influence and by their partner's flexibility and reasonableness.

Sometimes time and patience are the answer. Important problems aren't ignored. They are merely postponed until the environment is conducive to positive problem-solving and good communications. True changes may take time.

Be a good listener. Learn to put your own thoughts and strong emotions on the back burner while you truly attempt to understand your partner. Giving undivided attention is a gift of love. Listen when your partner is angry or upset. Listening helps the angry partner feel understood. Don't run away or avoid problems.

Be flexible and creative in your attempts to solve problems together. Negotiate, compromise, give in or propose solutions that benefit and satisfy both of you. Build trust by honoring your agreements. Live with integrity.

Conflict is good. Conflict shows engagement. Conflict gives couples a chance to clarify their own thoughts and emotions. If not confronted, it will grow and escalate. However, the process should be respectful and courteous. Couples need to have a plan in place to disengage when emotions are heated and to re-engage in the same discussion within a reasonable time frame.

Conflict resolution involves good listening, communicating clearly and not interrupting each other. It involves a willingness to compromise or to find solutions that work for both of you.

Commitments are honored after agreements have been made. This creates trust and a willingness to keep trying to improve the marriage. More needs will be expressed and more needs will be met. In this way the marriage gets better and better.

11. Be quick to apologize and forgive. Most people mean well. Couples don't generally act in deliberately destructive ways. In the heat of conflict, their misguided effort to quell conflict often is like gasoline poured on a fire already burning out of control.

Other actions will happen that are truly unfortunate, neglectful, mean-spirited, selfish and just plain wrong. Every relationship will have its emotional wounds and trauma experiences. Develop an attitude of resolving these issues quickly.

Marriage partners need to be able to apologize for offenses and be willing to forgive and let go of past hurts. Be quick to repair your relationship after conflict or hurts. Living with unresolved hurts and resentments takes an unseen and insidious toll on respect and love.

Try to learn about the impact of the mistake, acknowledge the harm that it causes, make amends if possible, ask for forgiveness and commit to preventing the hurt from occurring again. If you are on the receiving end, be quick to forgive. To forgive is a choice. Trust will be earned through time and change in behavior.

12. Seek spiritual growth and purpose. As a couple you need a common foundation of meaning, purpose and goals. Your shared spiritual understandings, commitments, and values provide the basis for cooperation and mutual effort.

The future means something. The way you live life means something. Striving for common goals and sharing common values will unify you as a couple. Having common goals doesn't mean being the same or doing the same thing. Each of you is unique. You need to identify and support your partner's personal goals, careers, chosen roles and ambitions. Helping your partner accomplish personal goals is an act of love.

Having children and raising a family deepens and extends your love. Sacrifice brings joy in your posterity and a love that extends across generations. Honor each other's family commitments and obligations. When all else fades away, your family relationships will be the constant fountain of nourishment. That's it. It's not easy. Having a great marriage takes a lot of work, but the rewards far out weigh the personal sacrifices involved.

Part II: Commitment

A successful marriage requires falling in love many times,
always with the same person.
- Mignon McLaughlin

WHY DO COUPLES STAY COMMITTED?
CHAPTER THREE

Why do some people stay married despite major troubles while others divorce because they feel they aren't as happy as they think they should be? Psychologist Carol Rusbult, of Free University at Amsterdam, has done research on this subject. She has found that the level of commitment depends on three main factors: level of satisfaction, size of investment, and the quality of alternatives.

Level of satisfaction. Couples experience commitment when important needs are being met and they feel attached to the romantic partner meeting those needs. Thus, the more a person "needs" the relationship, the more likely he or she will choose to remain. Despite the tendency of our individualistic culture to label dependency as bad, it is essential for successful relationships. What relationships need is interdependence, a voluntary and healthy form of dependency.

When there is a balance of power in the relationship, there is less opportunity for exploitation or abuse of power. Interdependence is the opposite of power. There is equality in their decision-making and each is able to influence the other. A relationship is pleasurable when couples cooperate. They become involved with each other's efforts and accomplishments and unselfishly give of themselves to each other.

Unequal dependency occurs when partners differ as to how

central their relationship is compared to other forms of life satisfaction. When both partners place similar value on their relationship, they allow more of their needs to be met and their mutual commitment grows.

We develop feelings of dependency and attachment when our partner:
- has similar attitudes and goals.
- has care and concern for our interests and well-being.
- is able to give empathic understanding, acceptance and emotional security.
- freely expresses his or her deep personal thoughts, feelings, fantasies, hopes and dreams.
- draws close to us with physical affection and sexual fulfillment.
- shows a strong liking for our positive qualities.

Ideas about what love is and how it is expressed influence our judgments on how satisfied we are. Feelings of satisfaction are influenced by the type of relationships we have experienced with past lovers, parents and friendships.

Investment in marriage. The value of a relationship grows with time. A couple accumulates a store of shared experiences that give their life meaning. The size of the investment binds couples together.

Over time, couples depend on each other's habits of thinking, expression and basic assumptions. They become increasingly accurate in anticipating and correctly identifying their partner's feelings and attitudes. The closer a couple becomes, the more they have memories in common. In this way, their identities actually merge.

More importantly, a person comes to view oneself on how their partner sees and responds to him or her. Personal identity is strengthened when couples share common meanings, perceptions and understandings.

Relationships blossom when partners give each other freedom, support and acceptance in helping each other grow and develop along unique paths. A partner's support and encouragement helps a partner express his or her best self. Their investment becomes an investment in each other. It grows as they aid each other in becoming the good and desirable person each wants to be. Their relationship has a history of the many reciprocal acts of love and personal sacrifice each has made for the other's well-being.

Social and cultural ties. The couple gathers mutual friends, shared financial commitments, possessions, children and in-laws. There are memories, love and obligations that are uniquely associated with their relationship. They bind each other together. The welfare of the children is a powerful inducement to maintain their marriage. Divorce is expensive in both financial and emotional costs.

Each partner also has a set of cultural and religious norms about the appropriateness of when and under what conditions a marriage should be dissolved. The strength of these norms and the social costs of violating them are a consideration in keeping their marital vows.

Quality of alternatives. In the past, couples in unhappy marriages went to great lengths to work out their difficulties. Now there is less tolerance for abuse, alcoholism, chronic conflict, and infidelities. Even so, divorce is bleak and daunting when one considers the economic and social consequences, especially when children are involved.

Abusive relationships, low income, low education, and no money on hand are factors in preventing women from leaving. Low self-esteem, reinforced by the abusive partner, convinces dependent partners that they are not going to get their needs met elsewhere.

There are periods when marriage satisfaction dwindles - when reality does not meet expectations. During these times of vulnerability, an attractive alternative may become a threat to a relationship. Couples with strong commitments ignore or minimize the attractive qualities of others.

Couples who are satisfied with their marriage minimize the attractiveness of others. They act constructively when their marital partner engages in an action that is potentially destructive to their relationship.

These couples minimize negative qualities or flaws in their partners. They redefine destructive past events in more benign ways. Finally, they keep a hope that the future of their relationship will be good.

PUTTING ON ROSE COLORED GLASSES
CHAPTER FOUR

I*married the world's most wonderful woman. Sorry fellas."* I
listened to my friend's statement and disagreed. I wasn't feeling
sorry for myself at all. I was sure I had married the world's most
wonderful woman. I'm sure that the vast majority of the men in the
room listening to my friend's bold assertion felt the same way.

How could all of us end up with the world's most wonderful
woman? It doesn't make much sense. I was glad my friend felt that
way about his wife and, given his attitude, felt assured that his
marriage would last. After all, who would want to leave the world's
most wonderful woman? Perhaps my friends and I are simply looking
at our spouses through rose colored glasses.

Why are rose colored glasses important? Psychologist Carol
Rusbult and her colleagues found that perceived superiority was a
key ingredient in long term, close relationships. Perceived superiority
is the tendency to view ones relationship as better than - and not as
bad as - other relationships.

Rusbult believes that people view their relationships as superior
because they wish or need to view them as superior. Commitment to
a partner is the chief motive for the tendency to put on the rose
colored glasses and see their relationship as superior. Perceived
superiority also gives people an optimism and confidence to continue
in the relationship because their goals and actions are likely to be
successful

People need rose colored glasses for those times when a
relationship is challenged and threatened. When couples experience
frequent conflict, they can focus in on the other good parts of their
relationship that excel.

Belief in the superiority of one's relationship enhances feelings
of security, certainty and trust. It helps people to persist during the
inevitable lows and hard times. The belief helps create the reality.
Positive illusions make it easier to sacrifice for and adapt to a less
than perfect partner.

Keeping healthy relationships is also important to personal well-
being. Relationships give individuals love, social support and
companionship. Having a rewarding relationship is a critical life
accomplishment that promotes happiness and self-esteem. On a

personal level, believing we have a superior relationship helps us feel successful.

Four ways to sustain commitment. Rusbult lists four ways putting on rose colored glasses helps sustain commitment.

1. Dependency. In a situation of low dependence, it is easy to see things the way they are - to acknowledge the good and not so good qualities of one's partner. In contrast, the more dependent you are on the relationship and the more you have to lose, the greater the need to see your partner in a positive and optimistic light.

2. Long-term orientation. With a long term orientation to the relationship, a partner isn't confined to the harsh reality of the "here and now." He or she can anticipate that better circumstances will exist in the future. This positive illusion is kept alive by imagining what might come to pass in the future.

3. Shared identity. Couples enhance commitment when they use the plural pronouns, i.e., "we," "us" and "our" instead of "I," "me" and "mine." What is good for the partner is good for the self. Committed individuals may develop a tendency toward perceived superiority because enhancing the partner is tantamount to enhancing the self.

4. Unconditional love. Strong commitment supports behaviors that build an unconditional relationship. Committed partners exert effort and absorb the costs of a relationship without counting what they get back in return. They also give unconditional acceptance to their partner - "warts and all." They translate their partner's faults into virtues or somehow see, yet deny, the negative qualities of the relationship.

Research findings. In their studies, Rusbult and her colleagues found less perceived superiority in dating couples who later broke up. This study and another study of young married couples showed that the higher the commitment, the greater the belief in the superiority of their relationship. For married couples, greater feelings of perceived superiority meant greater couple satisfaction and adjustment.

The responses of the more committed and less committed partners in a relationship were analyzed. It was found that the more committed partner exhibited greater tendencies toward perceived superiority than the less committed partner. This was done by enhancing positive thoughts and inhibiting negative thoughts about their own relationship, and by enhancing negative thoughts and inhibiting positive thoughts about other relationships.

Which comes first when couples split apart - taking off the rose colored glasses or questioning the commitment? Either way, once the glasses come off, the downward slide toward divorce or break up accelerates.

I'm still convinced I married the most wonderful woman in the whole world. Sorry fellas. I hope you can say the same about your mate.

WHEN THE BLOOM COMES OFF THE ROSE
CHAPTER FIVE

All marriages face disappointment. There is an inevitability to the struggle. The initial romance and passion fade. The press of day-to-day life takes over. Love doesn't conquer all. Marriage partners gradually come to realize that their differences are more important than they expected them to be - and that their spouse has characteristics less attractive than was imagined.

Why do some marriages last a lifetime while others with fewer troubles and differences don't make it beyond the first bump in the road? What happens when the bloom is off the rose?

A resilient response is a response from the heart, a mind set or a belief system about handling disappointment. It is a test of attitude, motivation, effort and strength of will to prevail in spite of obstacles in one's path.

Steve Wolin, M.D., from the Washington, DC area and author of *The Resilient Self*, finds the principles of resilience also apply to the way couples approach their marriages.

Spirituality/morality. The couple views their marriage as a sacred vessel, a third entity apart from their own needs and happiness. It is guarded and protected, nourished and cultivated.

Marriage is viewed as a commitment to each other, and a responsibility to the children, to the extended family, to the community and to God. Marriage is about honor. It is about adding extra layers of love and attention to cushion the disappointments that come hand in glove with marriage.

Regarding marriage as permanent promotes healthy boundaries and wise choices when confronted with opportunity and sexual tension. It is by personal integrity and spiritual commitment that marriage is protected.

Independence. This describes an attitude of generosity, of acceptance and even an ability to love rather than hate the differences between marriage partners. They show fundamental respect, understanding, forgiveness, or minimally, tolerance when confronted by a serious difference.

Partners do not have to be the same. "My partner is doing the best she can. I cannot ask her to be just like me." This allows for a sense of self, an ability to be separate, a space for individuality. Couples learn to be more tolerant about each other's faults.

Some irritating behaviors may be qualities that were initially attractive during the courtship. Differences are strengths and offer balance to the marriage. Even if they are seen as exasperatingly negative, couples learn to live with the difference.

Insight. A resilient couple isn't afraid of taking personal responsibility for their particular contribution to their marital problems. Both respond to the other. Both are worthy of blame.

Marriage partners look at themselves and acknowledge their part of a problem. By looking at their side of an issue, each partner can make amends and take constructive action without waiting for their mate to make the first move.

Initiative. Couples take a team approach to problem-solving. Each person makes contributions to solving problems during hard times. Marriage is strengthened when a couple faces and solves setbacks and life challenges together.

Couples appreciate the hard work they did as a couple to surmount the difficulty. "I didn't know we could be as effective as we are." As they go through life, they gain a sense of their competence and a sense of hope for the future. "Hey, we can do a lot together. Look at what we did." A team approach develops a sense of oneness and unity.

Humor. Resilient couples use humor to laugh at themselves and to break the ice when tension develops between them. It is an attitude of making light of their differences and regulating them to the realm of not being that important. "Here we go again, the silly fools that we are, messing up in predictably human ways."

The value of humor is that it minimizes the pain of disappointment. Humor shows an ability to detach and look at the big picture and to not let a disturbing difference take away from the overall good feeling a couple has between them.

Creativity. Wolin feels that couples can be creative in the ways they celebrate their marriage through special rituals and traditions. They create a shared identity as a couple. They recognize and take pride in the things they have endured together. They take pleasure in the contributions they make by combining their energy and ideas. Their positive accomplishments as a couple act to counterbalance and minimize their differences.

Relationships. Wolin believes that resilient couples see how freedom to pursue different experiences enriches their marriage. Marital partners encourage each other to go outside of the marriage and bring back information, energy, passion and ideas to make their lives better. Being a part of the community and drawing strength from it enlarge and enhance the marriage.

They grow individually because of their involvement with others and then return and share what they learn to strengthen their marriage.

Couples develop this set of resilient responses in the process of struggling over their differences. Something new comes out of the struggle that enables a couple to absorb the next shocks to the marriage in stride. That's why their marriages last.

Why Marriages Fall Apart
Chapter Six

If you're having marriage problems, the first and quickest way to solve them is to minimize conflict and eliminate the negative behavior. Drawing from my experience as a marriage counselor, here are ten common problems that keep love from flourishing.

1. Poor boundaries. Engaging in intimate conversations with members of the opposite sex leads to emotional experiences that cloud judgment, trigger fantasy life, and progress toward physical intimacies outside of marriage.

The connection and acceptance found in an illicit relationship diverts energy away from solving problems with one's spouse. Confiding about marital problems with a sympathetic listener provides a contrasting experience to whatever dissatisfactions might be present in the marriage.

2. Selfishness. There needs to be fairness in the distribution of work and responsibility within the relationship. This willingness to extend oneself also pertains to meeting emotional needs. Placing one's desires consistently ahead of a partner's emotional needs and responding only when it is a matter of convenience, demand or negotiations leaves a spouse feeling unloved.

If too many important needs are neglected over time, the unloved spouse feels used or taken advantage of. Consistent lack of love interferes with a spouse's willingness to give unselfishly in the relationship. When marriage partners don't trust their needs will be met, they tend to meet their own needs first and become hesitant to share freely of themselves.

Selfishness in its most destructive form involves control, manipulation, jealousy, possessiveness, demands and abuse in order to get one's way. In milder forms, it is lack of consideration and respect.

3. Disrespectful judgments. Marriage needs acceptance, admiration, appreciation and emotional safety. Feelings of anger and hurt follow when the process of exploring differences or contrasting opinions consistently degenerates into criticism, impatience, labeling, contempt, or discrediting one's thoughts or feelings.

It is disrespectful to try to change a spouse's thinking by lecture, ridicule, threats, brainwashing, or negative aspersions. These perceived attacks on personality, character, intelligence or values undermine the mutual respect that forms the basis of love. The tendency is to retaliate or else to withdraw and not share one's ideas. It becomes hard to love or give of oneself when one feels unfairly judged or mistreated.

4. Explosive, angry outbursts or rages. Anger can have a useful purpose if it is listened to and leads to dialogue and constructive problem-solving. However, anger can either create more anger or withdrawal, both of which interfere with effective communications.

Unbridled and unpredictable tempers interfere with emotional safety and trust when spouses need to engage each other on emotional issues. The issues behind the anger get lost as the angry response is perceived as unjust, abusive and unwarranted. It is intimidating and controlling.

5. Lack of emotional intimacy. The lack of sharing one's feelings, goals, hurts, struggles, joys and emotional details of one's life leads to loneliness and sadness. Feelings of friendship and partnership come from being connected through interest, deep listening and empathy, mutual support, and sharing perspectives as confidants.

Expectations for marriage include a desire for this soul-satisfying experience of being known, understood, loved, accepted and valued for who you are and having a place to turn for comfort and support. If this component of marriage is lacking, marital partners feel cheated of the essence of what they truly expect marriage should provide.

6. Lack of affection and sexual fulfillment. When needs for sex and affection are not met, problems mushroom. Without affectionate gestures and words, love seems hollow and not as believable. People don't marry to get a roommate. They expect to have an active and fulfilling sexual life. Chronic anger and conflict dampen a couple's willingness to be affectionate with each other.

7. Leading separate lives. Relationships also suffer when couples don't mesh their lives through shared activities, recreational companionship or time together.

Living too independently from each other takes away connection and joy from the relationship. Couples need to function as a team when it comes to parenting, managing a household, sharing finances, and relating to relatives. They need to consult with each other about important decisions and coordinate their schedules.

Time needs to be set aside to enjoy conversation, adventures, common interests, vacations and fun. Time spent together should be anticipated with pleasure. Without this component, couples drift apart and have little in common.

8. Communication is a painful process. A marriage with too much conflict, hostility, blame, criticism, defensiveness, and belligerent verbal attacks seems like life with an enemy instead of a friend. Marriage needs to be a place of safety, a haven, a place of love and refuge, not a war zone.

Always being "right," being rigid, judgmental, or easily angered or flooded with emotion disrupts communication before problems can be solved. Avoidance of conflict is even a bigger problem as the emotional connection is lost when couples don't share opinions and attempt to resolve conflict. When repeated attempts to solve problems fail, one partner gives up and starts to withdraw emotionally.

9. Destructive habits and addictions. Addictions have great power to be placed in front of the needs and happiness of a partner.

Betrayal, hurts, anger and pain follow the wake of addictive behavior. Addictions need to be treated to protect the integrity of the marriage.

10. Dishonesty, laziness and other character defects. Basic trust and respect underlie love and form the basis of relationships. Lies, deceit, disloyalty, secret habits, or emotional dishonesty about thoughts or feelings destroy trust and respect. Spouses who willingly don't take or follow through with their personal responsibilities unfairly shift those burdens to their partner. Marriage is a partnership between equals, not a parent/child relationship.

Part III: Dealing With Differences

Women marry men hoping they will change. They don't.
Men marry women hoping they won't change. They do.
- Bettin Arndt

WHAT DO MEN REALLY WANT?

CHAPTER SEVEN

Here are seven points of advice men frequently mention when it comes to describing what they would like in a marriage.

1. Be less critical. Men often feel they are on the defensive and "wrong" just for voicing an opinion that does not match their wives' expectations and standards. They want a feeling of teamwork, cooperation, partnership and a more legitimate discussion of issues in their marriage.

Accept him for what he is - imperfect. He needs to be accepted as he is with his own legitimate interests and hobbies. Take advantage of his strengths and good points. Men want appreciation for the things they are doing for the family. Reinforce and reward the things you appreciate him doing.

Don't make every issue between you a fight to the death. Some quirks and differences you can live with. Trying to change him adds to his and your frustration and resentment.

The home should be a refuge, not a place where he faces a barrage of criticism and conflict. How strongly and frequently you are judgmental of him may shut him down or trigger an emotional response that exacerbates the problem.

2. Forget the past. Husbands feel that some past hurts and blunders in the marriage aren't left alone. They feel matters they think are resolved are brought up unfairly in fights. "Let the dead stay buried." Forgive mistakes. Don't bear grudges. Don't bring up the past unless it pertains to a current problem.

3. Be supportive of work and leisure activities. Men want their wives to understand that work obligations occasionally take precedence over family needs. Some of their priorities are out of their control. "A man's got to do what a man's got to do."

Men would like understanding and appreciation for the work pressures and responsibilities they face. A man's work, accomplishments and struggles need to be recognized and supported. They also want acceptance for their occasional need to be alone or to pursue their personal interests.

4. Be nurturing. Giving emotional support, respect, admiration, attention, soothing and meeting needs makes coming home special. Family meals together give more than bodily nourishment. In homes where there is confusion, disorganization, anger or emotional distance, men don't do well. The family doesn't do well.

When women reject or struggle with the homemaking role, there may be a basic discontent that eats away at the marital relationship. These traditionally female responsibilities are important despite everything else that is going on in life.

This isn't a rehashing of stone age advice on how to please a husband - "shut up and wait on them." Mutual roles need to be clarified, understood and negotiated. If you are working outside of the home, this is a two-way street. He has a supportive role to play also. But the nurturing and caring still need to take place. What we are talking about is caring, not caregiving.

5. Verbalize needs. Men don't like being judged or criticized for not doing something they "should have known." There are times when they just "don't get it." They want their wives' expectations spelled out - the more detail, the better.

Don't expect him to read your mind. Be clear and spell out exactly what you want and expect from him.

6. Be a friend. Men want a safe haven, a best friend where they can unburden themselves and be accepted for who they are. They want to be able to share emotions and know their thoughts and feelings will be kept confidential. Companionship, affection and romance are important. They want a friend who can take their side and is supportive of their struggles.

Men have a much smaller network of friendships and support. There is much more dependence on their wives to be a sounding board and confidante.

7. Men like physical affection. Duh! Men make the romantic connection between feeling loved and physical intimacy. Women often feel that what happens in the bedroom is an extension of what is happening in the relationship. With men, what is happening in the relationship is an extension of what is happening in the bedroom. It is the same thing, only the emphasis is different.

If you really want to please him, occasionally take the initiative in lovemaking. The fact that you spontaneously show interest in him is more meaningful and arousing than most anything you can do. His sensuality is heightened when be feels that he is pleasing you.

The quality and frequency of a couple's sexual relationship may be quite satisfactory, but, from the male perspective, something is missing. A man doesn't have the feeling that he is wanted or desired for himself if it is always his idea.

8. Take responsibility for your own happiness. Don't expect your husband to solve all your problems. If you depend on him to make you happy, and always do the thoughtful, loving or right thing, you will be disappointed.

If you are insecure or unhappy with yourself, you'll have a tendency to put strong and unrealistic demands on the marriage. Over time, unhealthy dependency breeds hostility and resentment.

WHAT DO WOMEN REALLY WANT?
CHAPTER EIGHT

Husbands, do you wonder if your wife is ever satisfied with you? What do women really want anyway? By asking and then genuinely listening to your wife, here are some things you might hear.

1. Show emotions. Women want their husbands to know that the expression of emotions is OK. They want more emotional expression, more honesty, more feelings from the heart. Be willing to share your innermost thoughts and feelings with her - your joys, fears, doubts, worries and struggles. Don't let her have to pull feelings from you like a dentist pulls teeth. Intimacy created by deep communication is the type of intimacy that brings contentment to her marriage and makes sexual intimacies more meaningful.

2. Don't give lip service. Women don't like their husbands agreeing or placating them and then not following through. They want their ideas and concerns taken seriously. Women want validation that their feelings are important and their ideas have value.

Women don't like being put in the position of repeatedly requesting something and then being expected to be grateful when their husbands finally honor their request. To them it feels like begging and being rewarded - as if they were some sort of pet.

3. Recognize that differences of opinion aren't fights. Many wives have trouble getting issues talked about because husbands react defensively or angrily. Men may withdraw because of an emotional edge to the discussion. It is hard to get a legitimate discussion going about important issues. It feels like control when a husband won't address her concerns.

4. Understand family obligations. Women express concerns that their husbands need to be sympathetic and supportive of efforts to keep family ties with parents and siblings strong. Take an interest in family life. Attend your children's activities. Support, participate and join in enthusiastically in family celebrations and holiday traditions.

5. Negotiate work and parenting responsibilities. Fairness in family and household work is important. Resentments build easily if the workload in the family is one-sided. Your attitude about work in the home is about as important as the work itself. Women want a feeling of partnership and teamwork.

6. Show appreciation. Show appreciation and personal interest. Notice and compliment her for the many things she does to make your life and family life pleasant. Wives give a lot of unselfish love and service in the home and to the family. Her contributions need to be valued and recognized in a timely way. Women hate to be taken for granted.

7. Be generous with your time, attention and resources. Be sensitive to her needs and put her first, ahead of your favorite hobbies, and leisure pursuits. Be helpful by sharing in the household work and by being actively involved with the children. Nurture her. Make her load lighter. Being stingy or being too tight with the money without recognizing her needs doesn't feel like love.

Tune in to her needs and try to please her. Your willingness to go out of your way for her will influence her willingness to recognize your needs.

8. Be a responsive listener. Listen hard to understand your wife's feelings. Be careful not to give advice when all she wants is a sounding board.

Control your temper. Learn to solve problems without frequent expressions of anger. Having a track record for solving differences creates the trust necessary for other forms of intimacy to develop.

9. Be a friend. Do things together. Don't habitually put her in a domestic or mother role or the sexual partner role. Be interested in the details of her life. Cultivate shared interests, goals, conversation and genuine companionship.

10. Be sensitive when it comes to affection and sex. Women want to share affection without feeling obligated to respond with sex. Many women want to be more affectionate and loving in their marriage. They shut down, however, when they feel their husbands interpret any flirtation, affectionate touch, warmth, holding, cuddling, or banter on their part as an immediate invitation to roving hands and attempts at full-fledged lovemaking.

Female desire depends more on the context of a relationship. Much more depends on her mood, energy level, good feelings, absence of conflict and an element of romance than a direct physiological response to touch. Women don't want their lack of interest to be interpreted as rejection. Don't keep a scorecard on how often she responds. This kind of pressure and guilt isn't helpful.

A minority of women feel frustrated when their husbands don't show interest in love-making or affection. It is a challenge to their femininity and frustrates their own need to feel loved, desired or attractive in their husband's eyes.

Ask the question, "What do you really want?" and you'll probably hear more than you bargained for. By not asking the question, you will hear the answer come out in various ways as she attempts to tell you whether you want to hear it or not.

When it comes to women, there is always more to learn.

MY SPOUSE IS MY BEST FRIEND - OR USED TO BE
CHAPTER NINE

How well do you know your spouse? Do you really know your spouse? To answer these questions, answer true or false to the following statements:

I can name my partner's best friends.

I know what stress my partner currently faces.

I know the names of those who have irritated my partner lately.

I know some of my partner's life dreams.

I am very familiar with my partner's religious beliefs.

I can outline my partner's basic philosophy of life.

I can list the relatives my partner likes the least.

I know my partner's favorite music.

I can list my partner's major aspirations.

I know what my partner would do if he/she won the lottery.

I can relate in detail my first impressions of my partner.

I ask my partner about his/her world periodically.

I feel my partner knows me fairly well.

Scoring: If you answered true to more than half, consider your friendship to be an area of strength in your marriage. These questions were adapted from John Gottman's, *Seven Principles for Making Marriage Work.*

According to Gottman, successful couples have a "mutual respect for and enjoyment of each other's company." They are emotionally supportive and find their partner to be an emotional friend, a helpmate, and a soul mate. Couples "know each other intimately if they are well versed in each other's likes, dislikes, personality quirks, hopes and dreams. They have an abiding regard for each other and express this fondness" in big and little ways, day in and day out.

Negative thoughts about each other don't outweigh the positive ones. When couples disagree, they make frequent attempts to repair the damage. Their friendship helps insure that attempts at reconciliation are accepted.

What happened? The courtship began with attraction, intimate communication, fun, friendship and delight in each other's company. With increased knowledge, a young couple came to appreciate, admire and respect their partner's unique talents, gifts, values, courage and specialness. Then they got married.

But instead of a lifelong friendship, many marriages end up "sleeping with the enemy." The years come and go and so does the friendship. Where does friendship go? How does it get lost as couples live side by side and share the same struggles in life? How is it they stop sharing and learning about each other? How does admiration and respect turn into contempt and intolerance?

There is the obvious. Not enough talking or listening. Not enough time together. Not enough fun. Not enough goals in common. Not enough effort is put into bringing two worlds together. But that leads to emotional distance, not to hostility and painful conflict.

There is the less obvious. The couple's inability to resolve conflict in a respectful manner has a corrosive effect on the friendship. In their anxiety to win an argument or create the change wanted, they don't listen to each other. They react with anger, contempt, defensivenes and refuse to meet their partner's requests. Oftentimes they are unwilling to discuss the issue. They justify their anger.

They don't put the brakes on their negative comments. They are intolerant of differences and see their spouse's motives as deliberate and provocative. Neither partner feels understood or cared for. Friendship in marriage is killed off bit by bit through repetitive, futile habits of fighting. Gradually the negative interactions cause the partners to see each other as sources of frustration and pain rather than pleasure and support.

Men and women used to come from common backgrounds and had clear ideas and expectations of each other in the marriage. Expectations have changed. Traditional cultures and religious faith put a premium on family harmony. Overt expression of anger was discouraged - especially when the kids were underfoot, which they nearly always were.

Modern couples expect more emotional rewards from marriage. Couples express themselves more. There are more opportunities for conflict, more opportunities to negotiate differences.

A survey has shown that men and women share the following perceptions of who withdraws during arguments:

1. Men withdraw during arguments 42 percent of the time,

2. Women withdraw in the 25 to 27 percent range, and

3. Both withdraw in the 15 -17 percent range. In only 15 percent of the cases does neither one withdraw. These are couples who report having the best relationships.

Instead of withdrawing, what do these couples do? They keep their tempers under control. If they can't, they call timeout and agree to meet later. They take pains not to escalate a fight. If they see that hurtful comments have harmed their relationship, they are quick to try to repair the damage with positive comments. Most of all, despite their own discomfort and emotional arousal, they show empathy and understanding for their partner's point of view and allow themselves to be influenced by it.

Listening to each other's complaints and frustrations deepens their understanding and their friendship. Each knows their partner better and respects their differences as normal and natural. Being right and being married don't go together. Through respectful conversational etiquette, they avoid rip-roaring, name-calling, blow out fights that destroy friendship, trust and respect.

By learning how to handle conflict better, couples can get back to the basics of friendship and get to know one another. They meet each other's needs with kindness instead of being locked into an endless cycle of bitter infighting and recrimination. Their conversational style reflects the equality of their partnership.

Want your friendship back? Learn marital manners. You can learn communication skills that will help you be a respectful listener, speaker or negotiator in the face of your normal differences.

NIPPING MONEY ARGUMENTS IN THE BUD
CHAPTER TEN

Too many couples get bogged down in money arguments. No wonder! Money decisions represent ways people show what they value in life. Money arguments are proxy arguments for value discussions.

Is it alcohol and cigarettes? Is it fancy cars and fancy homes? Is it a lake home or a time share? Exotic vacations? Education? Savings? Retirement? Contributions to charity? Tithes to their church? Private acts of charity? Are they collectors? Passions, hobbies and compulsions show up in checkbooks.

Are people comfortable living on the edge or in debt? How aggressive are they in investing money to make money? Can they delay gratification and save for goals or do they carry consumer debt? Do they pay interest or collect interest?

How money is spent is a test of how a couple comes together in choosing a compatible lifestyle. It represents the merging of dreams, goals, ideas and values. Money matters force couples to really be a couple and to unify for common purposes. The decision-making process of who spends the money shows how power is handled in a relationship. Is it a joint decision-making process or does one partner arbitrarily make purchases without consulting the other?

Money is a test of loyalty and fidelity. Is there a pattern of deceit, lies, secretive spending, coverups, gambling or impulsive spending? Spending obligates both parties and incurs obligations or debt on both parties. Not adhering to an agreed on spending plan shows a blatant disregard for the feelings of one's partner.

It is betrayal. It is a violation of the marital boundaries. In some cases it rivals an affair in terms of the violation of trust that it triggers.

Prevention of money fights. If couples come to me with on-going money disagreements, I offer these guidelines that if accomplished can clear up persistent fights.

- Have an actual budget that functions as a true operating plan for spending decisions. Too many people say they understand the importance of a budget but don't take the time to sit down and deal with the reality of their money decisions. Too many couples, if they have a written budget, act as if it doesn't mean anything anyway.

Ignorance may be bliss, but it is also the blueprint for having repetitive money arguments instead of actually coming together to really solve the problem. Meet at least monthly to review your budget.

- Spend less than you make. You can't get by on a deficit budget. Some short term cash flow problems can be part of the budget, but basic expenditures can't exceed income. Greed and impulsive spending have to be curbed within the discipline of a budget.

- The budget needs to be realistic. Use actual data, not pie in the sky estimates. Discuss fuzzy areas, such as food, clothing, maintenance, entertainment, gifts, holiday spending, etc.

- Unify income and spending into a common framework. It is "our" income, "our" expenses, "our" savings, "our" debt, "our" investments, and "our" credit cards. Each is accountable to the other. Each is responsible to the other. It doesn't matter who makes what or who spends what or whether there are two checkbooks or one checkbook or one credit card or several credit cards if decisions are made through a single budget.

If you operate your money separately, you might as well be roommates or in a "living together" arrangement. Either you are a team and trust each other or else you are too independent. Picking and choosing which parts of marriage you like and which parts you don't like keeps the marriage from truly being what it can and should be.

- No secret spending. This is a violation of the marital bond. Addictions need to be acknowledged and treated. Seek professional help rather than violate money agreements in the marriage.

- Establish discretionary spending for each partner that is a part of the overall budget. Make it realistic. This is one area where you don't need to be accountable to each other except for living within the established amount.

- Have pre-established limits on spending that trigger an automatic joint-decision process before expenditures are made. Do this even if the resources are there to cover the expense. Honor your agreements. Expensive gifts, well meant, can be a violation of trust.

- If budgetary exceptions occur that jeopardize the overall budget, confer with each other on how to incorporate the expense into the existing budget. The same would be true for a "windfall" or an unexpected income that isn't included in the budget.

- Have emergency funds to cover three months of family expenses. Emergency funds give you peace of mind. Work toward this goal if it isn't possible at first.

Are you getting into trouble? The following are some "red flag" indicators of being overextended. These are taken from a book, *Till Debt Do Us Part,* by Bernard Podruska of Brigham Young University.

- Spending up to or beyond credit limits.
- No emergency funds.
- Making only minimum payments.
- Being unaware of the amount of debts.
- Making late or missing payments.

- Applying for additional credit cards.
- Refinancing or consolidating loans.
- More than 20 percent of take-home pay is used to make debt payments.
- Deceiving your spouse on the amount you spent or owe.
- Debts are turned over to collection agencies.
- There is no plan for avoiding debt, reducing living expenses or getting out of debt.

MONEY TRAPS FOR YOUNG COUPLES
CHAPTER ELEVEN

P artners in a new marriage have different backgrounds and ideas on how money is to be spent. It is an immediate test of their ability to communicate and work as a team in money matters. Add debt problems and sharp disagreements about how to handle them and tensions will rapidly escalate.

Common money mistakes. What gets young couples into financial trouble?

- **Expensive tastes.** They often finance a new car without any awareness of how much it is going to cost them in interest or how long they are going to have to pay. They also don't think about the insurance costs. When they figure out they can't make the payments, they can't get out from under it because they owe more than it's worth. They don't read what they are signing.

They have the same tastes as their parents and try to live just as comfortably. Besides a new car, they buy sound systems and new furniture - and go out a lot for entertainment. They can't afford it.

- **No clue.** They don't formulate a monthly budget and live within their means. They don't budget or save money for anticipated annual and occasional expenses. They have no idea what their total indebtedness is.

- **Credit cards.** They acquire three or four major credit cards (or more) and maintain high monthly balances. They borrow money on credit cards to pay current bills including housing and food expenses. They charge everyday expenses or small items and can't keep up with the monthly payments. They watch their charge accounts grow each month. They borrow more money before old loans are paid off.

Their incomes are stretched to the limit without any margin of error. Then something happens. Bam! They are behind the eight ball.

Taking control. Here are some ideas for young couples starting out on how to control money and, if necessary, dig themselves out of debt.

1. Have goals. Plan out expenditures so that spending fits within your means. Decide between wants and needs, and take care of your needs first. "Keeping up with the Joneses" and/or starting out with the same standard of living as your parents are dangerous practices.

Work towards something instead of buying now and paying later. Don't be seduced by our culture that says you have to have everything now. Convenience has a price. Don't saddle your future and your spirit with crushing debt.

Save for goals. Start small but be regular. Saving can be addictive just like spending. Saving is a habit. Use payroll deduction. Small investments early in marriage will reap huge dividends later.

2. Make a budget on paper together. Merge your incomes and expenses. Don't have a "his" and "her" money approach to finances. Negotiate each line item and come to an agreement. It doesn't matter who writes the checks as long you have merged your incomes and have agreed on the expenses.

Balance the checkbook. Spend time with the books. Shop for sales and bargains within your budget. Make a game of it. Figure in your occasional and annual expenses as well as your monthly obligations. Having a budget with goals builds in restraints on your impulse buying. Budget for discretionary spending for each of you. Set aside money for emergencies like job loss, accidents, illness, medical expense, and emergency travel.

Celebrate holidays, birthdays, and anniversaries with restraint. Put controls on gift-giving. Be patient. Someday you'll be able to afford the traditions you want. Establish controls over phone expenses.

3. Live up to your budget. Having one partner care about the budget and the other not cooperate or care about it sets up a parent/child dynamic and erodes equality and respect. Don't have secretive spending habits or hide bills. It destroys trust and security of the partnership.

4. Be smart about credit. There are two kinds of people - those who understand interest and those who pay it. Interest adds up and keeps you in debt. The minimum monthly payment on debts generally covers the interest with little reduction of principal. Having more than one major credit card can be a trap. Buying with a credit card is paying top-of-the-line interest. Look for a credit card with the lowest interest rate and low or no annual fees. Pay your bills as close to the due date as possible to avoid finance or late payment charges. Don't buy groceries or gasoline on a major credit card, unless it's paid off monthly.

5. Use discipline to get out of debt. Pay off one high interest loan and apply that payment to another. When one debt is satisfied, apply that payment towards another debt. Raises or additional income also can be used to reduce debt. Work from cash or money orders and use checks for mailing payments only. Keep track of expenses. Chart your progress. Be persistent. The first six months will be the hardest.

If you ever consolidate debt to get a lower payment, do not add new debt or you'll be in deeper than ever. Learn to live within a realistic budget or your loan consolidation won't do you any good.

6. Go for help. If you feel you have unmanageable debt, contact the Consumer Credit Counseling Service. They teach money management skills, work with creditors, consolidate payments, monitor your progress, offer encouragement, and treat you with respect. Marriage counseling may also serve to help you communicate better and sort out your differences.

HOW DUAL EMPLOYMENT AFFECTS MARRIAGE
CHAPTER TWELVE

Today employed women make up forty-eight percent of the work force. Forty percent of white, college-educated women earn as much or more money than their husbands. Young men's wages have been stagnant or declining for the past 30 years, forcing many new couples into dual income situations.

With all the changes in the past 50 years, what is the impact of dual employment on the lives of married men and women?

Psychologists Rosalind Barnett at Brandeis University and Janet Hyde at the University of Wisconsin - Madison reviewed research studies on how employment has changed men's and women's lives. Most of the effects described are positive, however, their review did not include the impact of dual wage earners on children.

The effect of multiple roles. Men and women who combine work, marriage, parenting and other family and community roles report lower levels of stress-related physical and mental health problems than their counterparts who have fewer roles.

For women, lower levels of distress are primarily attributed to their employment. Just as adding the worker role to women's lives contributes to their well being, men feel better about their lives when they participate in family life. However, employment for women with large families generally has a negative effect.

The positive effect of employment depends on the number of roles people have in their lives and the time demands of each role. Men and women are more than workers, parents and marital partners. They also function as friends, members of extended families, neighbors, students, or as members of church or community organizations. Research has shown that about five roles are optimal for well-being.

Marriage and stress. Even more important than the number of roles or time spent in each role is the quality of each facet of life. Problems at work, marriage problems or concern for children cause distress and anxiety.

A strong marriage is a buffer for work related stress. Both men and women rank marriage and parenting as more important to their happiness than their work involvement. By keeping friendship at the center of their marriage - even if it means sacrificing demanding job opportunities to do so - marital partners cope with their responsibilities and time demands.

Negative stress at work or in marriage is cushioned by success or satisfaction in other roles. The quality of family life lessens the impact of work related stress in men's lives. A woman's positive work and marital satisfaction can soften the stress of child care and the concern and stress of caring for elderly parents.

Women who moved into the workforce reported improved physical health and less depression. It is only when non-traditional women are employed more than 40 hours that the likelihood of marital disruption increases.

Flexible gender roles. Flexibility of gender role beliefs and behaviors are another key in managing work and family demands. The gap between the amount of time employed men and women spend in child care and household tasks still exists but has decreased dramatically in the past 20 years. The quality of the marriage depends more on flexible gender role expectations than earnings, relative earnings or occupational status of either partner.

Wives whose husbands were highly involved at home reported more marital satisfaction than those whose husbands participated less. Non-traditional men who engaged in active, involved fathering reported less psychological distress. Men with traditional gender role beliefs and less family involvement were more vulnerable to work oriented stress.

Additional ways marriages benefit from dual incomes. Besides buffering stress, dual income marriages benefit by additional income, social support, increased self-confidence, new ideas and more similar lifestyles.

1. Added income. Women who work bring in additional income and thus ease financial stress and anxiety. Among lower wage earners, men appreciated their wives tangible efforts to reduce financial stress. In recent times, men with decent incomes were not threatened by the amount of their wives incomes.

Marital conflict makes employment more attractive to home bound wives. Her additional income gives her more clout in the marriage and is helpful in working out a more equal relationship. The likelihood of divorce is greater for couples in which the wife had no income.

2. More social support. Work benefits women by providing a larger network of support. Women's well being is linked to social support from husbands, neighbors, supervisors and coworkers. Men's well being is chiefly associated with social support from wives.

3. Successful experiences. Work can provide opportunities for recognition and appreciation and a boost to self-confidence and self-worth.

4. An expanded frame of reference. Interaction at work offers opportunities for gaining more perspectives on the ups and downs of life. When men or women experience problems, they use these additional perspectives to cope more effectively.

5. Similarity of experiences. When couples combine work and family, their daily life experiences become more alike. They have more in common and more to talk about. They grow closer as they successfully work out fairness and cooperation in adjusting to the demands of joint parenting and performing household tasks.

COMING HOME FROM A STRESSFUL JOB
CHAPTER THIRTEEN

In today's time pressured world of two income families, how do families manage to find time and energy for their relationships? How do they shift gears from an aggressive, high powered work environment to the nurturing world of relationships and home?

This goes to the heart of our modern day dilemma - having quality relationships and family life while meeting the ever increasingly complex demands of the workplace. Here are nine tips to help you keep the fire of your personal relationship burning as brightly as the work you do.

1. Make your greetings special. Say with your body language, facial expressions, with the gleam in your eyes and your warm embrace that you are glad to be back in your loved ones presence. Listen with your eyes.

Take a few minutes to fill each other in on your day. Show interest and concern for one another. Coordinate your plans. Make your greetings special and you will establish a warm emotional tone for the rest of the evening. Take a few extra moments to unwind, set your attitude and be at your best when you hit the door.

2. Use the language of intimacy instead of the language of power. Shift your style of expression from the direct, competitive, action language of the workplace to the more indirect, conciliatory and tentative language of relationships. Your partner needs courtesy, appreciation, patience and acceptance. Take time to listen and to attend to each other's emotional concerns.

3. Show your love. Make a conscious effort to enter the nurturing role. Meet needs. Be kind, considerate and easygoing. Show by your actions and your words that you care for your partner and children.

Find ways of making life less difficult for one another. Find ways to please your partner. Be gracious. Be generous. Provide support for your partner when he or she is facing a crunch time at work. Express your love and appreciation. Give affection through touches and hugs.

Keep your sexual love vital and rewarding.

4. Share responsibility respectfully and fairly in the home. Do your part in helping to make the home and family run smoothly. Men especially need to be aware of doing their part with child care and housework. Roles and responsibilities need to be negotiated and divided so one partner isn't bearing an unfair burden.

These changes fly in the face of traditional gender roles and are not easy to make. Once new habits are formed, they will become increasingly easy and natural.

5. Simplify your life and lifestyle so that you aren't trying to do too much. Be clear about your values and what is reasonable in view of the many demands each of you face.

This world will have you do more and more. It is a world without limits, except your own. Much of the stress we bring into our lives is self-induced. Nobody can have it all, men or women. Temper your ambitions and desires to allow for the other part of life that brings much joy and meaning - the bonds of love, family and companionship.

6. When you are home, really be at home. Concentrate on the person or activity you are engaged in. Shift attention to the new situation wholly and completely. Don't try to do too many things at once. If you are preoccupied with something, schedule a time and address it rather than have it creep into your other activities.

Try not to bring work home. Manage your work life so that you address as many things as you can there instead of at home. If you do bring work home, coordinate with your spouse on what you need and when you plan to work on it. Outside of that time, really "be there" for your relationship. Discourage work related phone calls coming into your home.

7. Learn to enjoy leisure. Do exciting and new things together. Take breaks - three and four day weekends, mini-vacations, real vacations. Schedule and protect your vacation time from work demands. Learn to play and invite the child in your partner to come to play. Make memories. Have fun.

8. Keep communications alive. Give your relationship a chance. Structure time together so that meaningful communication can take place. Schedule walks together, breakfasts, lunches and a regular evening out. Plan a regular getaway weekend every three months.

Update understanding of each other. Learn something new about each other. Be curious about your partner's emotions, thoughts and dilemmas.

Track the changes they are going through and the challenges they are dealing with. Share feelings, hopes, dreams and struggles. Know when things are really right or wrong in your partner's life.

9. Find a work environment and a career niche that support family values. Choose your work well. Take control of your schedule. Assert yourself appropriately. Find role models, mentors and supervisors who care and support family life as well as work. Where you can, influence business attitudes and policies to be pro-family.

Special thanks goes to psychologist Wayne Sotile from Wake Forest University for his ideas and for his book, *The Medical Marriage: A Couple's Survival Guide.*

GETTING ALONG WITH YOUR IN-LAWS
CHAPTER FOURTEEN

I've given plenty of advice to June brides and grooms. Here's some for parents and their new son or daughter-in-law. As a by-product of the wedding, you inherit new family relationships. These relationships have the potential for tension and hurt. They can be respectful and accepting. Ideally, they are loving and rewarding.

Suggestions for the new son or daughter-in-law.

1. Don't try to strengthen your marital bond by attacking or undermining your partner's bond with his or her parents. Make your own relationship good and the loyalty issue will sort itself out. Don't try to shut off relationships. Everyone needs roots to live strong. Don't put your spouse in the middle with loyalty tests.

2. Accept your in-laws as imperfect. Be pleasant, easygoing and try to get along. Watch your nonverbal communication, too. Establish a relationship based on trust and mutual respect. Get acquainted, draw them out and be interested in their lives. Be gracious about gifts and hospitality.

3. You will disagree a lot during the first years of your marriage. Each of you has your own ideas on what the relationship should be like. Occasionally you'll put your spouse in the middle between your desires and the desires of his or her parents. Don't expect things to be all your way. Negotiate middle ground with your spouse regarding holidays, vacations, gift giving, family celebrations, frequency of visiting and amount phone calls. This will be a test of your ability to communicate positively and resolve differences.

4. Be a sounding board for your spouse. Don't create division and conflict by taking over his or her problem. Let your spouse work through his or her own issues. Be supportive.

5. Forgive any judgment or rejection from your in-laws that you may have experienced during courtship or early marriage when you were establishing new boundaries. Acknowledge any hurt you may have caused. Occasionally, you may want to resolve the conflict directly. Go to them and ask what they would like to see improved in the relationship. Don't go into a litany of past hurts and resentments. Focus on the future.

6. Your spouse is the best one to communicate with his or her parents about difficulties, problems or plans. Don't be the heavy. Unify first and then let your spouse be the spokesperson in resolving conflict or establishing limits. He or she will have more credibility.

Suggestions for the mother and father-in-law.

1. Don't be too critical or rejecting of a steady boyfriend or girlfriend. One may end up being your son or daughter-in-law. They will remember and perhaps resent your attitude toward them. Your own child may harbor anger about the way you handled the courtship.

The boy or girlfriend may have actively sought to subvert your authority and been disrespectful. In either case, hurtful things may have been said, remembered and remain unresolved and unforgiven. Be willing to talk directly with your new son or daughter-in-law to resolve past hurt or conflict.

2. Accept your son or daughter-in-law as permanent and support the marriage. Side with your child only if there will clearly be a divorce. Then you can go back to being their primary support system.

3. Be patient. If you have unresolved conflict with your child, let him or her mature and work it out in his or her own time. Acknowledge your mistakes. Time to work on autonomy at the expense of your relationship may be needed.

If the in-law is acting out his or her unresolved parental conflict with you, don't over react. There's plenty of time for the in-law to figure out that you are different. Your child will notice and help correct the problem.

4. Stand back and let the new family come to you with problems or advice. Be slow to comment on their affairs unless they encourage discussion. Even then, be a listener and don't be quick to give advice that they might resent. Don't interfere as they work out their differences. Define your boundaries when you feel they are taking you for granted. There are positive ways to help adult children without shouldering their responsibilities.

5. Prepare yourself to let go and accept the loss of closeness and control. You'll lose some closeness you've had with your son or daughter. That is a major loss, but your child's primary loyalty should be to his or her spouse. You now play a secondary role in their lives.

6. Be clear about what you want in the way of family events and visits. Negotiate and be accepting of your married children's decisions. Be friendly, hospitable and let them set the tone for how much closeness they would like. Avoid guilt trips.

7. Enjoy family time together, especially with your grandchildren. The safest and most positive way to be in their lives is to focus on the grandchildren. Take your married children's lead on how much to give the grandchildren. Ask first. Respect their different lifestyle and parenting style.

Honest communication and respectful boundaries will set the stage for family bonds that will grow as the family enlarges. Family events and relationships take on new meaning as both families continue a happy, harmonious journey through life.

Part IV: Love Takes Work

True love is not so much a matter of romance as it is a matter of anxious concern for the well-being of one's companion.
- Gordon B. Hinckley

LOVING ACTIONS CREATE FEELINGS OF LOVE
CHAPTER FIFTEEN

What is love? Love is an overpowering feeling, an intense romantic high and unbounded passionate desire for the presence and affection of our loved one. Right? Wrong! Romance is not love. Music, song, movies, popular culture, advertisements, literature and poetry encourage us to believe that love is a feeling. These feelings are real and are based on the excitement and passion of a new relationship along with feelings of awe, admiration, sexual attraction and acceptance. That part is true but it is only the beginning of love.

There is a predictable period of disillusionment that is as normal as was the rose-colored beginning. The newness of the relationship has been replaced with discovery of irritating differences and annoying habits.

Your partner isn't perfect. A partner's faults are the mirror images of the same qualities that provided the initial attraction. There is competition to see how decisions are made. Each partner brings with him or her powerful expectations from their childhood about what marriage should or shouldn't be like.

This awkward time tests communication skills and the ability to see and accommodate to a partner's needs and point of view. Giving love requires cooperation and yielding autonomy for the well-being of another. The demands of marriage are multiplied by the addition of a child. New challenges emerge as well as realignment of priorities.

Love takes work. If commitment to marriage were based on romantic feelings, then naturally the assessment of the marriage would be quite different from the days of its blissful beginning. At this point and throughout the coming decades of marriage, passion isn't the driving force though it should remain a delightful constant.

Love is action - a willingness to attend to another's well-being and nourish the relationship despite personal priorities or feelings. Marriage now needs to be sustained by daily loving acts of thoughtfulness, consideration, generosity and helpfulness. This practical side of love takes work, courage, effort, concentration, commitment and acceptance.

Love is a choice. In India, researchers studied the difference between couples who married out of romantic love and couples whose marriages were arranged. Couples in love-based marriages reported a decrease in their feelings of love after five years.

By contrast, couples in arranged marriages felt more love as the years went by. After 10 years of marriage, the arranged marriages were reported as more loving than the marriages formed through romance. Why would that be? Perhaps couples who believe love to be a feeling didn't extend themselves to create love by their own loving actions. They took love for granted - something they shouldn't have to work for.

On the other hand, couples from arranged marriages knew from the start that loving actions would be necessary to create feelings of love in their partner. Their conscious decision to love each other came because that was their only choice.

With time, loving actions created feelings of love. Part of those loving actions include affectionate and sexual touch along with deep sharing and confiding. Besides creating feelings of attraction and passion, loving actions create feelings of satisfaction, contentment, trust, mutual support and understanding.

We choose to love by:
- Doing fun things together.
- Making life less difficult for our loved one. We show love by doing our fair share of work in the house and with the family.
- Sharing decisions through mutual respect, negotiations, and compromise.

- Not escalating a fight or retaliating when it is well within our right to do so.
- Giving affection and intimate physical touch in the context of a loving relationship.
- Listening and giving an understanding heart to a partner's feelings.
- Sharing private hurts, dreams and joys of life.
- Being compassionate in giving potentially hurtful concerns and criticisms.
- Supporting and encouraging a partner's growth.
- Expressing love, appreciation and admiration for your partner's special qualities, gifts and thoughtful actions.
- Soothing and comforting your partner when he or she is under duress, facing a crisis or going through a loss.
- Protecting the marriage from competing relationships by being loyal even when there are marital problems.

What if we don't feel love? You can change the way you feel by how you act. When you act in loving ways, with time you will come to feel great love, empathy and compassion toward your partner to whom you are showing love. If there is a discrepancy between the way you feel and act, feelings will catch up and mirror your actions, not the other way around. If you wait for your feelings to change before you start to act, your feelings may never change.

"What we serve and what we learn to love takes our time, and what takes our time is what we love." -Marvin J. Ashton

In the long run, it is what you choose to give your time, attention and resources to that will be the true measure of what you really love. People who enjoy great prestige, power and wealth can still maintain equality and love in their marriage by loving and giving generously to their loved one. If you are genuinely serving your mate, it is hard to be cruel, arbitrary, selfish or high-handed.

Be the first to love. It is easy to love someone who is loving you. If you start loving first instead of holding back, you can change the relationship. Consistent love over time also changes the way people perceive and feel about us. The pathway to love starts with simple, sustained actions.

A woman lamented the actions and attitudes of her husband. She judged him harshly and felt he was the big stumbling block in her happiness. She decided to be unconditionally constructive - to unilaterally turn on her warmth, charm, love and go out of her way for him for six weeks.

Later, much chagrined, she exclaimed, "It must have been me! He's changed completely. He's responding in a loving and sweet way. It must have been my attitude that was causing the problem."

A relationship can change even faster when two people both try at the same time. Each partner magnifies and appreciates the effort the other one puts forth. They tend to minimize or discount their own actions as not being important. But they really are important to their partner.

Love is as love does. Love is a choice, not a feeling. Giving love creates feelings. Being loved creates feelings - feelings of love.

MARRIAGE FLOURISHES WITH SACRIFICE AND DEVOTION
CHAPTER SIXTEEN

How much time and attention do husbands and wives devote to meeting their own needs versus meeting the needs of the other? Here are five different attitudes that will help you rate or judge your commitment to your spouse's well being: selfishness, convenience, fairness, sacrifice, and devotion.

1. Selfishness. When a relationship is based on selfishness, satisfying your own needs becomes a top priority. The needs of your spouse are seldom taken into account. A relationship based on selfishness is about taking and getting rather than giving.

Selfishness represents a trust in power to get your own needs met. A spouse acting in a selfish way doesn't trust their partner's willingness to give what the other wants. However, you can't really use power to make people love you or want you to have what you want. It doesn't work. Behind the illusion of control in selfishness is helplessness.

2. Convenience. Relationships based on convenience occur when one partner is allowed limited access to the other's time and attention. The needs of the partner are sometimes considered, but only when it is convenient to do so. This is often expressed as, "I'll be good to you and do things for you as long as it doesn't inconvenience me."

Partners are willing to be helpful but are reluctant to sacrifice. The subtle message, "You are not a top priority," is sent. A spouse learns that he or she is not that important to their partner, at least not as important as he or she wants to be. After time, a spouse who feels like a second fiddle may seek importance in other places, such as in a job, children or friendships.

3. Fairness. A committed relationship is based on a willingness of each spouse to share what they have with each other through bargaining, compromise and negotiations. There is a willingness to solve problems. There is trust in the basic fairness and equality of the relationship. Each partner is vulnerable to the other, trusting that his or her partner will not exploit a willingness to give or inconvenience oneself for the other.

Reciprocity is the basic minimum for a good relationship. There is balance in the relationship. Your needs don't take precedence over your partners' needs. The willingness to give is tempered by reality. Discussion, negotiations and give-and-take are important skills in insuring that both partners' needs are being met.

In the short term, one partner's needs may take precedence but over time both partners' needs will be met in a balanced and fair way. There might be tradeoffs but no score keeping. The logistics of life require a good relationship to be good at problem-solving and compromise, not just sacrifice.

4. Sacrifice. This kind of relationship is based on a willingness to give without regard to equality or expectation of return. Sacrifice has caring as a foundation. Each partner experiences pleasure in meeting the needs of their partner. Your own needs don't matter as much as pleasing your partner or putting your partner's happiness first.

This willingness to respond to a partner's needs may also be described with words like love, service, and charity. To give in this way involves a commitment of time, attention and resources to meet another's needs even when it is inconvenient. Your needs are willingly set aside to meet the needs of a loved one. By reaching outside of yourself through acts of love, you affirm the value of the one you love.

5. Devotion. When a relationship is based on devotion, each partner actively seeks opportunities to serve the other. Instead of waiting to be asked, each spouse tries to anticipate the needs of the other and to meet those needs before they arise.

This is an active, vigilant monitoring of their partner's happiness. It is similar to the way a host monitors and anticipates a guest's needs before they ask. An example would be, "I thought you might need some time alone, so I took the children to the park."

In a marriage, devotion means knowing your partner well and being mindful about him or her - giving yourself over wholly and purposefully.

It doesn't matter that much whether the loving action is a result of willingly responding to a request or anticipating a need. It shouldn't be a source of conflict. This takes a change of heart from "getting" to "giving" and in centering one's attention on the other's happiness.

Desire to change. Increasing the amount of giving in the form of sacrifice or devotion increases intimacy. Occasionally there might be an act of thoughtlessness based on convenience or selfishness.

On the other hand, mediocre relationships generally center around fairness, convenience or selfishness with only occasional acts of sacrifice and even fewer acts of devotion.

Couples in poor relationships need to make a courageous decision to become vulnerable to the love and good will of their partners for getting their needs met. The miracle is that we get love by giving love.

(This continuum of five attitudes is adapted from Bernard Poduska's work on resource allocation within marriage. He is an associate professor of family life at Brigham Young University.)

MAKE YOUR GREETINGS SPECIAL
CHAPTER SEVENTEEN

It is a little secret of life that can make a big difference. This habit will add extra joy to your life. It will connect you with those whom you love and make you special in their eyes. This secret will make you many friends. This secret can transform an evening or a life.

Make your greetings special. That is the secret! "What?" you ask, "That is too little of a secret to make such a big difference."

We have a need to belong, to feel connected with those who are special to us, to share our lives and find someone who delights in our presence. The daily hassles and even the storms of life shrink when love and companionship create a citadel of friendship and refuge.

Every day brings separation. Each has a different journey - work, errands, meetings. There's always something new - new thoughts, worries, excitement, sadness. In ways that are entirely healthy, couples venture out from their base camp of love and security, deal with the world and come back together.

In the first two to 15 minutes when a couple comes back together, they need to communicate this message to each other:

"We are a couple. We care about each other. Our relationship is important. I am interested in you and what has happened to you since we've been apart. Your happiness is important to me. What you have been doing matters to me. Your life is important. I care about you. What is on your mind? Now that we've been apart, how best can I meet your needs?"

How do you do this? Eye contact. A big smile. A warm embrace. An affectionate touch. All this nonverbal communication takes place in the first few seconds a couple is together. The nonverbal expressions are more important than the words that follow. It is a great start. Without it, the words that follow are empty.

Next, the couple gives each other undivided attention, active listening, enthusiastic interest, genuine concern and helpful support. This exchange of feelings and thoughts may take just a few minutes depending on the circumstances. It can happen in the kitchen as both work together to get the meal going.

Children need special greetings too, sandwiched between Mom and Dad's conversation. They can learn to wait for more undivided attention once Mom and Dad have finished talking. Or they can be given a warm greeting and then sent on their way. "This is Mom and Dad's time together. I'll look at your school project in just a few minutes."

The initial few seconds and minutes are the most important. After the greeting, each is free to attend to the children, to prepare the meal, to attend to the orderliness of the home, and to find a few moments of rest and relaxation. If nothing is done to bridge separate worlds, the stage is set for miscommunication, impatience, irritability, selfishness, defensiveness and loneliness. With a warm greeting, a lot of unnecessary tension can be avoided.

People need to shift gears from the competitive and time pressured world of the workplace to the world of meeting needs and emotional intimacy. If people are stressed out and in a poor mood they need to take an extra 10 or 15 minutes to set their mood before coming home. A warm greeting two hours after the fact leaves a lot to be desired.

After a warm greeting, their renewed bond gives each the respect and freedom to be and do their own thing without feeling irritated or threatened by their separateness. The same behavior after a positive greeting will be judged differently. The context has changed. They reconnect as a couple, reinforcing the love and shared lives they lead. Those few moments of togetherness lighten the load and put all the stress and hassles back into perspective. Someone cares.

A warm greeting can set the emotional tone for the whole relationship. A series of warm greetings repeated day after day, week after week, can set an emotional tone for the relationship. They bridge their two worlds and fill in the gaps. They know one another and don't get very far apart.

The longer a couple has been away from each other, the more important and enthusiastic the greeting needs to be. Harm is done by a flat and unresponsive greeting after a long trip. It is like a cold slap in the face.

People put energy into their farewells and communicate the same message of togetherness when they part. Saying goodbye in a special way reassures the other of the special ties they share. It is insulting to have someone go without a farewell. Couples need to acknowledge their comings and goings by this common courtesy.

Try this simple secret. It takes practice to establish new habits. It isn't hard - not rocket science. It's a fun habit. Say hello with a gleam in your eye and warmth in your voice and you'll have sparkle in your marriage.

RITUALS GIVE VITALITY TO MARRIAGE
CHAPTER EIGHTEEN

T*he biggest threat to good marriages is everyday living.*" - Bill Doherty, Director of the Marriage and Family Therapy Program at the University of Minnesota.

There are a lot of pressures in our society that make intimacy and mutual enjoyment difficult. Couples are busy with work, individual pursuits, parenting, consumerism, and entertainment. It is easy to become too busy or distracted to give their relationship the time it deserves. If couples are too passive, it is easy to give their marriage short shrift among all the other things going on in their lives.

Couples don't realize how intentional they need to be about nurturing their marriages. Time needs to be set aside for conversation, recreational companionship and physical intimacy. Doherty suggests consciously developing "connection rituals" to insure that couples stay emotionally connected as friends and confidants.

Rituals are defined as significant social interactions that are repeated and coordinated. These are the times when couples share time and attention with each other. These rituals are important to maintain.

Examples of connection rituals. What are some of the marriage routines that are coordinated, repeated over and over and have emotional meaning?

Activities such as scripture study and daily devotions, mealtimes, running errands together, date nights, walks, working in the garden, greetings, farewells and setting aside special times to talk are examples of connection rituals. Celebrating anniversaries, birthdays and other special occasions are rituals. Rituals are predictable, coordinated and done with enthusiasm.

A lack of meaningful heart-to-heart conversation is probably the biggest drawback to keeping a relationship warm and intimate. Here are some ground rules for effectively making time to talk to each other on a regular basis.

- **Have a clear transition.** A ritual is easier to enact when it is anchored to a part of daily life like breakfast, greetings at the end of a workday, after dinner or at bedtime. Without a pattern, the time will be inconvenient and difficult to coordinate.

- **Make it enjoyable.** Avoid talking about the logistics of living and family life. Don't use this time to solve problems or work on relationship differences. If it is about logistics, then it isn't personal. If is it about problems, then it is work. If it is about conflict, then it is unpleasant.

The goal is to enjoy each other's company. The conversation is between emotionally connecting friends who are being curious about each other.

- **Have a clear ending to the ritual.** The time spent should be predictable. If not, negotiating the ending time will involve struggle and detract from the pleasantness of the experience. Twenty minutes a day is a good place to start.

- **Be regular.** If you have to miss a time, mentioning that fact will show that you both value that time together. The ritual is good for the relationship even though occasionally one partner may not be personally "up" for it. If travel, family demands or other intrusions interrupt the ritual for a while, get back to it or you'll lose it.

What do you talk about? Creating the ritual is like setting the scene and creating an atmosphere for talking. Couples need to ask each other open-ended questions about the bigger issues of their life, the same way you would if you were meeting a friend you hadn't seen in a while.

"How is work going?" "What is it like for you when...?" "How are your parents doing?" "What do you look forward to next year?" "What is your biggest challenge right now?" "What do you see yourself doing in five years?" These kinds of questions express interest in what is going on with each other's life and feelings. Be curious. Don't assume you know what is going on. There is a huge depth of information to learn about each other if we ask the right questions.

The way you listen to each other is important. Be prepared to listen and show loving interest in the topics your spouse brings up. Be relaxed, prepared to ask follow-up questions, show concern and be a patient listener.

Poor listening involves analyzing the responses or disagreeing with them. Those are conversation stoppers.

Sex as a love ritual. Sex also has to be repeated, coordinated and significant. Spontaneous sex can be great but there is too much opportunity for confusion and conflict. The marriage needs sex - not just when each partner spontaneously feels like it.

Couples should approach sex like an affectionate greeting ritual. You do it anyway whether you feel inspired at the moment or not. Sex is personal but it also serves as a connecting ritual. Marriage needs sex whether the individuals do or don't at the moment.

The lack of a common bedtime routine is a detriment to marital affection. It is a part of the coordination that makes lovemaking possible. There needs to be predictable regularity to sexual relations with appropriate signals, transitions, favorite times and comfortable situations.

The best of both. According to Doherty. "Love and intimacy rituals are like regular sex and special sex; the first is a familiar and reliable companion, the second you can get yourself prepared for but it always feels like a gift."

Doherty is the author of *Take Back Your Marriage: Sticking Together In A World That Pulls Us Apart.*

"YES, DEAR"

CHAPTER NINETEEN

A minister told the prospective groom in a premarital counseling session that there were some special words that he should use with his wife. If he spoke them, she would always love him and really make him happy. He further told the young man that he should tell these words to her in the bedroom, in the kitchen, in the car, in the store and when they were out on walks together. The young man thought to himself, I know these words, "I love you." The minister then said, "The words you need to say are, 'Yes, Dear.'"

The minister's advice has been corroborated by research findings on the ingredients for a successful marriage. Basically, it boils down to this. If a man shows his willingness to respond to his wife's concerns, go out of his way to please her and to aggressively meet her needs, she will in turn respond in positive ways to the things he needs or wants.

Why can women be so hard to get along with? If a wife isn't able to count on her husband to be considerate, loving and generous with his time, energy and concern, then she is more than willing to contest with him in a battle of the wills. She does this to establish her influence in the marriage and to get his cooperation on things that are important to her. She wants to be taken seriously. She wants to be cared for and served as well as to be the giver of love and service.

"Yes, Dear," within the framework of a mutually agreed on budget, can be said in the store, with home furnishings, with clothes, with children's needs. "Yes, Dear," can be said in regard to home repair and improvements. "Yes, Dear," can be said about a night out, family vacations, visits to family and holiday plans.

If a man will give in on the little things and adopt an attitude of putting his wife's needs first, even if the scales seem unbalanced, he will find that he hasn't given up a thing in terms of decision-making on the bigger issues in their marriage. A pattern of "Yes, Dears" will promote genuine negotiations and accommodation when he wants his needs and desires taken into account.

Why aren't those words said more often? Many men have an expectation of entitlement and male prerogative about who is to serve whom in a marriage. This may have something to do with past gender roles where the "breadwinner" worked long and exhausting hours. He would return to the comforts of home where his wife assumed the lion's share of the work and parenting responsibility. Not much was expected of him.

Perhaps these words are not said because of pride and stubbornness. Maybe it comes from an archaic notion of male dominance. Or is it because men think that by being compliant they are giving up power? Could it be something from their family background where their basic needs weren't met? Are they so needy that they have a hard time giving love when they haven't felt loved?

A habit of love. By saying, "Yes, Dear," or words to that effect, a man develops an attitude and habit of love. He practices setting aside his agenda, his convenience, his need to be right, and his need for his wife to do things his way. This is an experiment in sacrifice, of consistently putting someone else ahead of himself.

The nice part of this experiment is that the service you give is returned in kind. Love creates love. It is easy to love someone who is loving you.

Why men and not women? Why should it always be the man to lead out with this service? In modern marriages, a wife is just as likely to be in the workforce. She arrives home equally tired and exhausted. She is looking for her husband's support and involvement with the homemaking and childcare duties. His willingness to pitch in - to lighten her load and to share the work - is a sign of his love and devotion. She sees her demands and expectations as reasonable.

She does her part, generally more than her part, but expects a cooperative attitude in dealing with the home front. In her estimation, the little things count. That is why, "Yes, Dear," is music to her ears. She also likes to be noticed and appreciated for the things she does, but that is another story.

What goes around, comes around. However, when she encounters resistance, argumentativeness, indifference, laziness and self-centeredness, this is a battle she is willing to engage. Such behavior, too much, too often, calls into question whether she is being loved. She, in turn, can be just as difficult, self-centered, demanding and argumentative. In addition, she can be angry and judgmental when she feels she has to fight to have her needs met. He sees it as her problem and then wonders where the love went. "Yes, Dear," eliminates all that and sets her free to be warm, nurturing and giving.

Is this too one-sided to expect husbands to be the ones to be this accommodating? Perhaps, but if you think of it as balancing the scales for all the loving service a woman gives in a family, then it isn't one-sided at all. In the long run, men who are attentive to requests and needs receive more love back as they give.

TIME TO BE AVAILABLE
CHAPTER TWENTY

In the world of work, we are bold, courageous, tough, persistent, energetic, and goal-driven. We do what has to be done. We confront obstacles head on. Time is valued. Effort sustained over time brings results.

These values are assuming greater importance in our competitive world. These are the bywords of success. *"The power of applying attention, steady and undissipated, to a single object, is the sure mark of genius."* - Chesterfield

By themselves, these values are not enough. The hard-driving work values need to be balanced by values that nourish and sustain the human spirit. Too many organizations fail to use the talent available to them. Too many marriages suffer from a lack of attention. Too many children grow up without enough parenting.

Values of the human spirit. In the world of relationships we are generous, nurturing, available, accepting and compassionate. These values put people ahead of things that have no life. Time is of no consequence. We become aware of the needs of others and meet them.

There is time for love if our goals, self-importance and our self-imposed deadlines haven't overwhelmed us. Many people do not "listen" with their heart because they might have to take time to act upon what they might "hear."

The clock rules. Life is a race to the finish line. We run with a delusion. We believe there is not enough time when there really is. We shut down the soul to win the race.

With our expressions and behavior, we hang out a "Do Not Disturb" sign so others will not bother us. Then one day, we wake up to the fact we've been winning all right - but running in the wrong race.

Our race with the clock dehumanizes us. E.M. Forster noted, *"The people I respect most behave as if they were immortal and as if society were eternal. Both assumptions must be accepted if we allow a few breathing holes for the human spirit."*

Theologian Martin Marty makes a similar point. *"...It takes a sense of eternity to make one realize that there is time, time to be available and to create."*

If we believe that, then there is enough time for ourselves, our work and for others. We are not threatened when things don't happen to go the way we think they should.

Interruptions are not "bad." Things don't always have to go according to schedule. We can still accomplish our goals and still care about others. There is time. Plenty of it.

This doesn't need to be an either/or situation. The busiest and most accomplished people know how to concentrate on the present precisely because they are organized and in control. Neither do they neglect themselves. They allow time for personal growth and self-renewal.

These individuals protect their work time. They use wisdom in judging between the demands of their own priorities and the times when their schedule can and ought to be set aside. They avoid over scheduling themselves. They are available to attend to others when needed.

Take the time to listen. People who make themselves available to others know how to listen. And they take the time to listen. They are genuinely interested in others - and it shows.

Their concern is more than words. They want to help others. They signal with their eyes, face and posture that they are approachable.

With a tilt of the head, a bent ear or a light in the eye, they say, "For this moment or for however long it may take, I am at your disposal. I am not afraid. In fact, I welcome whatever you may say."

I have met people like this. They are an inspiration. They aren't too busy or too caught up in themselves. Part of their attraction is that they do not discriminate. They are willing to be engaged and signal that willingness to everyone.

Others, from whom I expected better, didn't share what they could have. No matter what their accomplishments, I was repelled by them. They communicate their emotional distance.

The best employers, supervisors, husbands, wives, fathers, mothers, and friends are willing to take time and give of themselves in both planned and unplanned ways.

They radiate their availability. Their window has a candle in it for the weary traveler. The door to their soul has a large welcome mat in front of it.

When you think about it, we can measure what we value in life by keeping track of that to which we give our attention. Attention is the ultimate personal gift; one we don't have to give. No one can order us to give attention to something. It is a choice.

If people are generous with their money and miserly with their time, have they given that which is most precious? Not yet. When people are generous with their time and attention, they are truly generous.

Love and time form a bond. Sharing time is a another way of sharing self. What we love takes our time. There is enough time for love. There really is.

SHORT COURSE ON ROMANCE
CHAPTER TWENTY-ONE

Unromantics, here are some ideas that will save you the trouble of peeking in women's magazines at the magazine rack to supplement your meager gifts of expression and lack of imagination.

The luster of romance. Like it or not, Mr. or Mrs. Unromantic, your spouse is probably an incurable romantic. By some mysterious law of nature, the unromantics and romantics seem to pair up. At the risk of being politically incorrect, I would guess that women desire romance in their life more than men, although I've seen many times where the male is the frustrated romantic in a relationship.

Most romantics don't think it is romance if it is their idea. This is something they hope you discover on your own. If your romantic partner has to coach you on how to do it, it takes the fun out of it.

Short course on romance. Romance blossoms in the rich soil of the unexpected. Romance is spontaneous, unpredictable and unhurried. It is fun.

A one word definition of romance is "surprise." Not just any surprise, but a surprising way to show your loved one that you cherish and value his or her presence in your life.

It is the unexpected thoughtfulness, the surprising gesture of love, the perfect gift, a love note left to be found, a bouquet of wildflowers, a prearranged babysitter and a surprise night out. It is an overnight trip for just the two of you. It is the thoughtfulness that goes into the surprise that makes it even better.

It is playfulness in the kitchen and in the bedroom. It is letting your loved one know that he or she is attractive and desired. It is a mood and atmosphere of love, the care in which the stage is set, and the extra effort made for the perfect touch. It is sexuality cloaked in mystery. It is male and female discovering each other anew. It is the unexpected moment of being cherished by one who loves you.

Everyday love. One caution. Don't put the cart before the horse. Without the everyday experience of being loved and cherished, gestures of romance will not be appreciated - they may even be resented.

Love is the expression of attitudes and behavior in which the well-being of our loved one is first and foremost in our minds. Our happiness is not complete without his or her happiness. This loving consideration is expressed in many ways - in the constancy of daily actions. The big things are the little things. The lift and loveliness of life comes with daily doses of kindness, consideration, courtesy, thoughtfulness, affection and appreciation.

What is love? It is greeting your loved one in a special way. It is offering a helping hand. It is giving personalized attention. It is being patient with imperfection. It is remembering special occasions. It is communicating with an affectionate touch or a knowing glance.

It is listening with an understanding and caring heart. It is giving comfort in time of need. It is sharing innermost feelings and expressing one's love. It is heartfelt recognition and admiration for what your loved one does and who he or she is.

It is the desire to please and to know how to please. It is acknowledging the gifts and love that are so freely given to you. It is putting your loved one first above all else and all others.

AFFECTION: THE MORE, THE BETTER
CHAPTER TWENTY-TWO

Between married, engaged or courting couples, affection is a nourishing reminder of how special and important each is to the other. It is the way couples habitually regard each other, both in terms of mindfulness and acts of thoughtful consideration. Affection that is expressed ritualistically and not daily doesn't carry much weight.

"Affections are our life. - We live by them; they supply our warmth." - William Channing

Affection defined. Other words for affection are loving and tender gestures, showing warm regard, fondness, partiality, holding dear, cherishing, keeping or cultivating with care, holding in one's mind deeply and resolutely, devotion and ardent love.

These are action words, feelings that are expressed publicly and privately. Affection can be deliberate and articulated or it can be unconscious and automatic. It should be both. Affection is about little things. Affection is about constancy. It is not about display. It can't be turned off and on. It has to be real or it doesn't mean anything.

"Affection, like melancholy, magnifies trifles; the magnifying of

the one is like looking through a telescope at heavenly objects; that of the other, like enlarging monsters with a microscope." - Leigh Hunt

How can you recognize an affectionate relationship? Most children grow up with an awareness of whether their parents were affectionate with each other or with themselves as children. It is a lot of little things that add up. **Affection is:**

- **in the eyes,** in the way they look at each other with glances of adoration, delight, of mutual understanding or obvious concern.

- **in the smile,** in the welcoming approach, in an enthusiasm that radiates and is not self-conscious.

- **in the desire for touch and to welcome touch,** to be near, to embrace, to hug, to hold hands, to reach over to rub or caress, and within the bounds of privacy to give and welcome playful intimate touch.

- **to prefer each other's company,** to find ways of being together, to share a private world that others only glimpse.

- **to sacrifice,** to put each other first, to generously give of oneself when it is inconvenient, to extend oneself at one's expense.

- **to be receptive to requests** and respond willingly and enthusiastically.

- **to anticipate** and meet the loved one's concern or need before he or she thinks about it or asks.

- **to think and plan** ahead with their partner's happiness, delight or pleasure in mind.

- **to listen intently** and really know their partner's needs and desires - and then surprise him or her with the perfect gift or gestures that demonstrates that intimate knowledge.

- **to find occasions to express love,** admiration and appreciation for the love a partner gives. This can be through cards, gifts, and written sentiments.

- **to celebrate each other** and the relationship on birthdays, anniversaries, holidays with recognition of how special he or she is.

- **to express love through intimate touch** in an affectionate and mutually satisfying sexual relationship that deepens the affectionate bond only the two can share.

- **to be utterly devoted and mindful** when there is misfortune, tragedy, setbacks, harm or threat of harm that places the loved one's well-being at risk. It is to be there for each other.

Learning to be affectionate. Some people are more apt to act this way when they grew up receiving affection and were made to feel comfortable when giving it. Parents show their love through affection. They also model affection in the way they interact with each other.

But what if this isn't in their background? It is something to overcome. It goes beyond affectionate touch, however. It is getting used to freely loving and putting another ahead of oneself. I liked the definition of "keeping or cultivating with care."

People can learn to be affectionate. They need to practice it daily, get comfortable with it and make it a part of who they are. It will take effort and focus at first.

Couples who live their lifetimes together grow in affection as their bonds deepen. It is a delight to see older couples express pure affection for one another in their maturity.

"Mature affection, homage, devotion, does not easily express itself. Its voice is low. It is modest and retiring, it lays in ambush and waits. Sometimes a life glides away, and finds it ripening in its shade. The light inclinations of very young people are as dust compared to rocks." - Charles Dickens

Sex gets in the way. Sexual communication and affection are often confused. If affection is shown only as a prelude to sexual desire or if the timing is not respectful, then it is fended off. Overall affection is a necessary context in which a good sexual relationship can flourish.

Affection is so much more than sex. It is a thing in itself and the more of it in a relationship, the better. With a clear understanding about the intent and appropriateness of affectionate touch, a couple can be free to express as much affection as they want without it being misinterpreted or rejected.

"There is in life no blessing like affection; it soothes, it hallows, elevates, subdues, and bringeth down to earth its native heaven: life has nought else that may supply its place." - L. E. Langdon

Part V: Emotional Intimacy

*Oh, the comfort, the inexpressible comfort of feeling safe with
a person, having to neither weigh thoughts, nor measure
words, but pouring them all right out - just as they are-
chaff and grain together, certain that the faithful hand
will take and sift them and keep what is worth keeping,
and with the breath of kindness blow the rest away.*
- Dinah Marie Murlock

BECOME AN EXPERT ON YOUR SPOUSE'S EMOTIONAL NEEDS
CHAPTER TWENTY-THREE

It is one thing to want to please a spouse and another to actually do it. How many times do we think we are doing or saying something wonderful only to have it be unappreciated or have it turn out to be the wrong thing? Often the goal of pleasing one's partner gets lost in the pressures of life or in our own self-centeredness.

Needs are not identical. In some important dimensions people are attracted to each other's opposite qualities. There are important gender differences, differences related to family background, and different expectations of what it is to feel loved and cared for by one's partner.

One common mistake is to assume that our partner's needs are the same as our own. We mistakenly try to please our partner in the same way we hope our partner would please us.

In his book, *His Needs, Her Needs*, psychologist Willard Harley,

Jr. of White Bear Lake, Minnesota advocates that marital partners become experts at knowing and then persistently devoting the required effort to meet their partner's needs.

I often have couples take this test. How well do you know your partner's emotional needs? I ask them to listen to a list of emotional needs being described and then have them guess which would be their spouse's top three or four needs.

Each spouse identifies what their actual needs are versus the guesses of their partner. The discrepancies are interesting and can be the basis for getting to know one's spouse better.

This list is in no particular order of importance. Put your spouse's initials in parentheses beside what you consider to be his or her top three needs and have your spouse do the same. After you do that, initial your own needs. Then discuss the results.

1. Physical attractiveness. This is usually important in courtship and may continue to be an important value. If your partner has gained or lost a lot of weight since marriage this could be a concern. Being pleased by your spouse's appearance in public means something. Some spouses are finicky when it comes to grooming, cleanliness and good taste.

2. Emotional intimacy. This is the feeling of being connected to your partner. You talk, share feelings, and turn to each other for comfort and consoling. You stimulate each other by sharing ideas and perspectives and by using each other for a sounding board as you process thoughts and feelings. You feel you have a best friend who is there for you. You feel free to say what you want to say without feeling judged or criticized.

3. Recreational companionship. You count on your spouse to do things with you. You want to do things together, to have a companion, to share some of the same interests and activities, to have fun and find enjoyment in each other's company. It could be as simple as being in the same room or as complex as having high adventure vacations or a shared hobby.

4. Sexual fulfillment. Your sexual needs and desires are an important aspect of love, sharing and pleasure. You feel connected, desired and loved. You want your spouse to care about this aspect of your relationship and to have regular and reasonably predictable sexual relations.

5. Affection. You like the expression of love and caring shown in a variety of ways including touch, hugs, kisses, embraces, appreciative and endearing glances, cards and gifts, expressions of love, warm greetings and loving actions that cushion life and relieve burdens. The composite of these actions is obvious to you and others that your partner loves you and wants to be with you.

6. Honesty and Openness. You value trust, honesty and openness in your relationship. You want to know important emotional details of what is going on in your spouse's life and what your spouse really thinks and feels. You trust his or her word and commitments.

7. Admiration. You want your spouse to recognize your positive qualities, to notice and appreciate your talents and to feel you are special. You want your spouse to recognize your value and the contributions you make at home, at work and in the community.

8. Domestic support. One aspect of domestic support is to share equitably in household responsibilities, child care, family activities and obligations, holidays and special occasions. You want a partner who is a team player in making the home a functional and pleasant place to be. You want the home to be a place of peace and relaxation where you feel supported and encouraged.

9. Financial support. You want your partner to be a team player who cares about the financial well being of the family and the future. You care about the budget, savings, spending and making ends meet. You have financial goals and want your partner to care and support your efforts.

10. Career support. You want your spouse's care, concern, interest and support as you manage your career and work life. You would like your spouse to be a valued sounding board for the challenges you face and to show recognition and appreciation for your accomplishments.

11. Family commitment. You want your spouse to actively care about family events, children's activities and obligations. This may also include family devotions and church involvement. You also want your spouse's support when it comes to your relationship with your own parents, siblings and to attend family gatherings.

How did you do? Are you an expert - or not?

Barriers to Intimacy Take a Heavy Toll
Chapter Twenty-Four

What is wrong with these marriages? **Partner A commutes during the week, comes home and parks himself in front of the TV.** He takes little interest in doing things with his wife or children. He acts like he doesn't want to be bothered. He asks few questions and shares little in return. His wife is starving for physical and emotional intimacy and some activities together.

Problem: Self-centered laziness. Couples marry because two people can be happier and survive better together than apart. If only one person's needs are being met, however simple they may be, their partner grows resentful. Marriage takes work. It takes an active commitment to pleasing one's partner and putting his or her needs ahead of one's own. Meeting needs is a sign of love.

Couple B fights too much. They argue and bicker. Affection falls off because of the amount of anger in the relationship. They become guarded in their personal feelings. It isn't safe to talk - except to criticize or to blame.

Problem: Their lack of intimacy is brought on by their inability to accept negative feelings and differences in their partner. They have lost the trust and goodwill to share their innermost feelings and hurts. They need a way of communicating that is courteous and respectful.

Partner C is touchy, angry and keeps to himself. He withdraws and nurses grudges when his wife tries to bring up issues. Conflict is too hard and painful. The partner who wants to talk gives up and hides her true and honest feelings from her husband. They grow apart. They live parallel lives and talk very little except about the children and the mechanics of life. Their children leave home and their common purpose in being together weakens.

Problem: Failure to respond to the concerns of a partner gives a message of a lack of caring and love. It is hard to trust someone who you believe doesn't care. It is easier to find friends and keep busy with work, the family and other people. They grow apart with their busy lives. With an empty nest, their companionship isn't enough. They haven't been close nor have they found enjoyment in each other's company. During a time of crisis, one partner may feel abandoned because of the perception that his or her partner wasn't emotionally there for them.

Partner D has an irresponsible habit. Despite pleadings and entreaties, she is unwilling to do anything about it. Her partner loves her and cares about her but is frustrated by the effect her habit has on their relationship and the family. He grows weary and gives up trying to change her. He loves her but doesn't respect her. Their relationship takes on a one-sided father /daughter quality.

Problem: Lack of respect for a partner who doesn't face up to his or her personal responsibilities takes a toll on intimacy and affection. Love and passion die out when a spouse is perceived as another child in the family. It is hard to turn to a partner for confidential advice and emotional support when you disrespect the way he or she manages life.

Couple E are busy professionals. Their worlds are too far apart. They put their careers ahead of their marriage. They don't switch from the powerful, competitive atmosphere of the workplace to a helpful, cooperative and nurturing partnership in the home. They are competitive with each other. They struggle with issues of fairness and equality in the home.

They are edgy with one another. When they are on vacation they manage to enjoy each other, otherwise they are too distant and self-preoccupied. They don't need each other except for those special times.

Problem: It takes time to nurture a relationship. A marriage has to be put before work, at least enough so that there is time and energy given to their relationship. Couples have to learn to give and sacrifice for one another and know that it works. If your partner's needs are being met, he or she stops keeping score. If your needs are being met, you stop keeping score.

Couple F doesn't talk enough. The husband is close-mouthed and guarded with his feelings. He finds it difficult to listen to his wife and puts her off by his impatient "fix-it or shut-up" attitude. He doesn't understand how just talking about a problem with a caring listener may be all that is wanted.

Problem: Intimate conversation is a valued and strong expectation of marriage. It is easy to feel cheated and short-changed with a marriage that is cold or indifferent to personal expression.

The lack of emotional intimacy is painful. It may lead to a lack of physical intimacy, which is also painful. One partner may be vulnerable to an affair, especially if it involves an understanding "listening ear." This will contrast with the stale, defensive communications in the marriage.

Keep the bond alive. If couples have an emotional bond or connection, they still have the will to solve problems that get in the way of their relationship. They work hard in counseling. They can apologize, forgive and put the past behind them.

Without that bond, marriage loses its vitality. Discouragement sets in. People grow apart. They grow more critical of each other. They become less affectionate. Arguments are more intense. Silence becomes a way of life.

If any of the scenarios above sound familiar, fight through the barrier that is robbing your marriage of the intimacy it needs.

KEEPING INTIMACY ALIVE IN YOUR MARRIAGE
CHAPTER TWENTY-FIVE

Do you remember the days of your courtship? Remember the easy flowing conversation? Remember how you exchanged private and intimate thoughts about your past, your struggles, and your hopes and dreams? Do you remember sharing your hurt and pain, the joy, excitement and the silliness and seriousness of life?

Try to remember the inside jokes, the shared view of the world, the private vocabulary and brutal honesty that you saved for one another and no one else. From your unique vantage point, you looked out and saw the world in remarkably similar ways. No one was allowed to invade this realm of privacy reserved for just you two.

Yes, those were the days of wine and roses. Those were the days of being intensely fascinated by the details of your loved one's life. You freely shared your world and took the risk of allowing yourself to be known. There was pleasure in knowing and accepting your loved one just as he or she was. This was not a time of imposition or projection but a time of exploration and discovery.

Together you opened the floodgates of the heart and let the essence of yourselves flow freely. You trusted that the good and beautiful would be prized and cherished while the bad and ugly would be faithfully discarded with kindness and charity.

Marital relationships are built on trust and confidences. The human spirit needs a release for the cry of the heart, pure acceptance, safety and trust that what is said is truly confidential. We need confidential relationships - at least one. A hidden blessing of a tragedy is that, perhaps for the first time, a person learns to turn to a confidant to bear his or her soul.

"If we are truly prudent we shall cherish those noblest and happiest of our tendencies - to love and confide." - Bulwar

In marriage, family life, and best friendships, we expect that our character, struggles and secrets will be respected and protected. The hurt of being betrayed by one who is close to you and one who truly knows you, destroys faith in human nature and puts up walls that are not easily broken down.

Love, trust and sharing confidences go hand in hand. It is a risk we take, a dangerous path to follow. Yet, without venturing on that path, we deprive ourselves of love, wisdom and total acceptance by another human being.

"To confide, even though to be betrayed, is much better than to learn only to conceal. In the one case your neighbor wrongs you; but in the other you are perpetually doing injustice to yourself." - Simms

People can be too safe, too cautious and deny themselves the love and support that is available to them if they would only open their mouths. If people are to err, it should be in trusting too much rather than too little. Honesty and truth, even if painful, opens the door of the heart. A spouse is honored by the trust that is placed in them.

Problems grow in marriage when communication is poor. There is too little understanding of one another. Each person wants to trust and love but their differences keep them apart.

Too many spouses grow wary and frustrated when they are not listened to and understood. Too many spouses are too indifferent or self-absorbed to try to understand another. Sometimes the process of trying to understand one another is too painful because of poor communication skills.

So what happened? Why are you so distant? Why are you now afraid to share your life? Why are you no longer curious to know the details of your partner's thoughts and emotions? Where is the intimacy you once had? How can you get it back?

Here are some typical problems that take away intimacy along with some suggestions on what to do about it.

Problem: Too much conflict over differences. The easy acceptance was lost as you merged your lives. Fear and frustration in solving problems lead to a retreat from honesty and a mistrust of your partner's willingness to see your needs or position as legitimate.

Anger, criticism, rejection, hostility, indifference or failure creates this fear to listen and understand. Contempt, criticism, defensiveness or a lack of willingness to engage the problem take a destructive toll on motivation to try to solve problems.

It is too hard. It is too painful. You stop trying. Communication breaks down. Lack of honesty and open expression are casualties of the unhealthy conflict.

Solution: Create a safe haven for expression of needs, fears, pain, frustration, doubts, anger, and differences of opinion. How people talk about their differences usually determines how they feel about one another. The process has to be pleasant and respectful.

Really listen and hear what is being said with your defenses down. Be as selfless as possible when listening to your partner. Screen out your own emotions and needs while focusing intently on their feelings and ideas. Be intuitive. Put yourself in his or her shoes. Take your partner to a deeper level of understanding.

Be a sounding board as he or she explores his or her reality. Don't intrude in this process by imposing your own judgments, opinions, arguments, assumptions, or preferred explanations on the flow of ideas. Encourage more disclosure, more and deeper honesty by your understanding. Patiently wait your turn to express yourself. Be tactful, tentative, conditional and exquisitely gentle in the way you talk about problems. Show an awareness that there are two opinions that matter and that differences are legitimate and solutions are to be negotiated. Conversational manners count more than you think.

Problem: There is not enough time for each other. This is a crazy, stress-filled world with too many demands, distractions, and counterfeit values that rob relationships of the time they deserve. By being too busy or too wrapped up in your own separate lives, you subtract time, energy or attention from the relationship that means the most.

Solution: Be clear about your priorities. Love takes time. Love takes companionship and doing things together. Having time together won't happen unless you make it happen. Something else will have to give. Find time for fun, for playfulness and for humor. Find time for affectionate and intimate touch, for vibrant and pleasurable love making.

Love takes talk, a lot of talk. Talk about the future. Talk about your goals. Talk about today and tomorrow. Get back to being curious and learning about the details of each other's everyday lives, concerns and joys. Build and share your private world. It is amazing to me how couples can live together and not really know each other.

Problem: Not enough personal kindness and love. Why be intimate with someone who doesn't love you? Couples who retreat to selfishness and meet their own needs first undermine their happiness. Love is putting your partner first by meeting needs, faithfully and consistently.

Either through anger, hurt or inertia, you no longer look for ways to please your partner. Not enough energy or awareness goes into ways of showing love and concern. It is too easy to be unkind.

Solution: Go out of your way to express your love and appreciation in loving gestures and actions. This takes thoughtfulness, cooperation and awareness of what brings pleasure to your partner. It is easy to love someone who loves you. Be the first to love.

Loving deeds have to match words. Commitments need to be honored. It is then that you will trust your heart and your feelings because you trust the love coming to you.

WHO PAYS ATTENTION IN RELATIONSHIPS?
CHAPTER TWENTY-SIX

Who pays the most attention in relationships, men or women? To women, the answer is obvious. They do. Some men might dispute this, but they don't have a clue. Why would women be more attentive? Historically, women have needed to be accurate perceivers of men because of the difference of status and power between the sexes. Men generally had greater power to both reward and punish women than women had over men. Consider these points.

- Women in marriage or romantic relationships pay more attention to men. They are more accurate perceivers of how men see themselves than men are about how women see themselves.

Men are more influential in courtship and marriage and therefore do not need to know their partners as well. Research has shown that when the quality of the relationship is disregarded, women are the same as men in predicting self-perceptions. However, when it came to happy marriages, a series of studies showed that the women's adjustment depended more on the women being accurate about men than vice versa.

- Women in courtship more readily confirm men's view of themselves than vice versa. Several studies show that confirming a man's self-concept is associated with good courtship progress or marital satisfaction.

The opposite case of a man confirming a woman's self-concept had little or no effect on relationship satisfaction. Success involves massaging a man's ego by seeing him the way he sees himself. Men seem to have more concern for their self-concept being validated than the need women have for validation from their marital or dating partners.

- A husband's emotional maturity and mental health are more vital to a wife's marital adjustment than are the wife's emotional maturity and mental health. Research shows women to be greatly affected by their spouse's personality problems while men ignore or are more tolerant of their wives' neurotic tendencies.

One study found that a husband's marital distress or depression caused depressive symptoms in the wife. However, the reverse wasn't true. In unhappy marriages, a man's mood affects the wife's mood more than vice versa.

What are the implications? To some men, intimacy means relating to their partners how they feel and what they need. They expect women to focus on them and their needs. Traditional women in courtship are much better than "liberated" women in decoding men, confirming their egos, and accepting the pace of courtship dictated by them. During courtship a man may become emotionally expressive, but once his partner is secured, his interest in interpersonal interaction falls off.

After marriage, he appears to be satisfied if his wife is a good sexual partner, is physically attractive, can bear and manage children and maintain an attractive home. He doesn't need to understand her. He's got everything he needs. Presumably, he could be married to almost anybody and it wouldn't make much difference. On the other hand, what a man thinks, his moods, his personality, and his problems make a great deal of difference to a woman's happiness.

A wife wants understanding, recognition and interest in her feelings. Sadly many men don't respond soon enough to correct the one-sided nature of their relationship. Marriage has changed with the entry of women in the work force. When incomes become equal and traditional sex roles are blurred, men become much more perceptually accurate, sensitive, intimate and cooperative.

As power between the sexes is equalized, the old rules are going by the board. Courtships are a lot more rocky and problematic. The same is true with marriages. Women want and expect more. Men learn to pay attention when they have to. As men become more empathic and caring about women's thoughts and feelings and aggressively meet their needs, their relationships improve.

How can men develop this sensitivity to the details of their partner's life - their personality, moods, feelings and thoughts? They can do this by being curious, patient, interested listeners. A good listener communicates care and concern. Receptive body language is important. Eye contact is important. Paying attention to the non-verbal cues their partner gives them helps them track the emotional content of what is being said.

One of the biggest mistakes men and women make is not really listening. Instead they formulate their own ideas and responses while the other party is still speaking. They think they are listening but they are not.

A fast radio commercial can be absorbed at about 100 words per minute. We have the capacity to actually listen to up to 140 words a minute. What do you think our minds are doing while the other person is speaking, especially when we think we know what they are going to say anyway? Thinking ahead, thinking of our rejoinder, that's what.

By being "right," argumentative, or inattentive we overlook a lot of what is being said. When men or women work at being better listeners, they get to really know their partner. They care more about each other's lives, and work more in harmony with one another.

What Is The Deal On Men and Intimacy?
Chapter Twenty-Seven

Why do men struggle so much with emotional intimacy? What does research say about men and emotional closeness? Psychologist Richard Osborne of Saratoga Springs, NY, has summarized research on various questions about males and intimate relationships.

Do men engage in fewer intimate relationships than women? Yes. Women have more same-sex friendships and they are longer in duration than male friendships. There is more personal sharing and exchange of support. Male friendships are focused on shared activities and interests.

Beginning in the college years, men are most likely to name a woman as their best friend or confidant while women are more likely to name another female. Men's social isolation increases as they move into middle and later age.

Are men different than women when it comes to self-disclosure, expressiveness, and even non-verbal behavior? Yes. Men self-disclose less than women. Men hide their weaknesses while women conceal their strengths. Adolescent males are less likely to share negative judgments and feelings about themselves than their female counterparts.

Men are less proficient at recognizing feelings, either their own or other's. Men are less expressive with their faces than are women. Men are less likely to sustain eye contact and avert their gaze. They maintain greater physical distance from others. They smile less. Their voices are less soft, fluid, pleasant, and less varied in pitch. These nonverbal behaviors and voice quality play a role in communicating empathy. This lack of expression is in spite of the fact that as infants males are more emotionally expressive than females. Also, both in infancy and childhood, no differences were found in the amount of smiling between males and females.

Researchers suggest that males begin to respond to "display rules" - cultural standards about the quality and quantity of emotions that can be expressed in different contexts - as early as age six.

Do men and women handle conversations differently? Studies show men are more dominating and controlling of conversation with women while women are more supportive and deferential. Women pay more attention to emotional tone and relational status (rapport talk) while males focus on informational content (report talk).

Males withhold feelings and information as a means to establish or maintain control in relationships. Women withhold feelings and information to avoid personal hurt.

Why do men avoid intimacy? Men avoid intimacy when they feel emotionally vulnerable. Oftentimes intimacy is seen as a threat to autonomy and masculine identity. By sharing deep intimate feelings, some men may perceive themselves as weak and not in control.

Men, unlike women, spare themselves the vicarious stress, emotional pain and obligations that come from being empathetically connected to others. Emotional distance also helps keep a problem-solving focus.

These reasons, coupled with withholding as a power tactic, are why the threat of intimacy is perceived as outweighing the benefits it provides through support, validation and emotional release.

Does lack of male intimacy cause problems? Males with low intimacy are more stressed by life transitions and change. One study found that males who were high in intimacy had higher positive life adjustments 17 years later.

One reason males are thought to die younger is because of the lack of social supports in their lives and excess stress caused by habitual inexpressiveness and suppression of feelings. Men typically depend on their spouse or on their work associates for their social support. This leaves them vulnerable as they retire and lose wives through death and divorce.

Single, divorced and widowed men are more likely than either married men or their single female counterparts to experience a deterioration of physical and mental health. A woman's web of supportive relationships leaves her less dependent on marriage for emotional support. She is better equipped to seek support during times of stress.

Suppression of feelings and failure to confide lead to negative health results such as hypertension and other stress related diseases. Men tend to act out their emotional pain or stress arousal through risk-taking and aggression. They also manipulate or suppress their emotions through drug and alcohol use.

Research has shown that husbands feel far more understood and affirmed by their wives than vice versa. Sharing feelings and positive communications are the strongest predictors of marital happiness. A lack of emotional sharing is one of the main causes of women's greater unhappiness with marriage.

Poor health, poor mental health, social isolation, poorer marriages - these are steep prices to pay for avoiding intimacy.

EMPATHY OPENS THE DOOR TO THE HEART
CHAPTER TWENTY-EIGHT

Next to love, empathy is the best thing marriage partners can give to each other. It is the best gift you can give to an angry spouse. It is a comfort to your spouse when he or she is bogged down with heavy cares. It is a springboard to deep communication. Rob Scuka, Ph.D., a social worker and Director of the Couples' Programs at the National Institute of Relationship Enhancement in Bethesda, Maryland, shared with me his ideas about the power of empathy.

When we use this power:

Empathy reduces loneliness and helps another person feel validated, connected and understood.

Empathy helps the recipient clarify and deepen their comprehension of their own thoughts and feelings, their experiences, the world and social reality.

Empathy helps the recipient become more trusting, more open and honest in expressing their feelings.

Empathy communicates understanding and respect. The recipient doesn't feel the need to be defensive or attack you when you express your feelings.

Empathy helps the recipient listen to your side of a disagreement and work constructively on a problem. It fosters mutual understanding and compassion.

Empathy has the capacity to heal, the capacity to transform a relationship.

When we learn to use empathy:

The giver overcomes their tendency to judge and reject others. The giver becomes more tolerant and compassionate toward the feelings and point of view of others. The impact of what is being said is less personal and makes it easier to understand another perspective.

We overcome separateness and differences. It overcomes the human tendency to be self-concerned and self-centered and to transcend our self and understand the other person's inner experience.

We improve the quality of communication and problem solving in a relationship. We open the door for forgiveness.

What is empathy? It is the ability to set aside one's own preoccupation, feeling, thoughts, concerns and advice to focus exclusively on the feelings, concerns and desires of another. By doing this we become free to experience an issue from another's point of view. An empathic person also accepts clarifications and revisions to their response.

To become genuinely empathic we have to become as selfless as possible. It is a skill to be cultivated - to put our ego on the shelf, to put our own personal agenda aside, to pretend for the moment we don't exist so that we can focus exclusively and selflessly on the subjective experience of the other person.

Scuka affirms, *"Empathy presupposes that human beings are not intrinsically different from one another. Apparent chasms are bridgeable because we have the underlying capacity to identify with another's experience. At root we are similar."*

How can you give empathy? Follow the threads of what is given you. Amplify the implications of what is being said. Help the other person verbalize what he or she hasn't quite managed to say. Imagine the deeper emotional context of what is being shared and try to make explicit what is implicit.

Empathy is about absorbing the other person's mood and putting yourself in their place. It is asking yourself, "What would I be feeling? What would I be wishing or thinking of doing if I were the other person?" Empathy is giving voice to their most important concerns and feelings that they haven't yet managed to express.

Scuka explains empathy this way: *"I can make sense out of your experience. I have the capacity to enter into your experience from the inside out and 'become' you. Thereby I can identify with your subjective experience. To accomplish this I use myself as a tool. I use my own humanity to allow me to understand your experience."*

Empathy is different than active listening. Empathy is more than mirroring or reflecting back what the other person has said. Active listening can be accurate but not empathic.

According to Scuka, empathy involves reading between the lines to bring out and verbalize the unstated, but implied, emotional content of what has been said. "This is the 'gold standard' of empathy." To be empathic, a listener gives full attention, eye contact, and listens intently.

Don't call attention to the listening role by using "I" statements. A good listener uses direct empathic responses such as, "You feel . . .," or, "You're concerned about. . ."

Empathy is given only in a context of kindness and safety. It is that security that encourages further self disclosure. Heightened negative emotions such as anger reduce the ability to be empathic.

How do we learn empathy? By seeing and by doing. Seek out an expert and watch empathy being properly modeled. It can be learned like any other skill. You watch it being done, you practice it and then generalize it to other situations. Consider it a foreign language and approach it with the same diligence. It can be done.

By learning to be empathic, two people can begin speaking a common language - the language of the heart. Adds Scuka, *"It is by using this language of the heart that two people deepen their sense of intimacy."*

Part VI: Physical Intimacy

*You musn't force sex to do the work of love
or love to do the work of sex.*
- Mary McCarthy

AFFECTION IN MARRIAGE DEMANDS
THE RIGHT TOUCH
CHAPTER TWENTY-NINE

How important is the physical expression of affection in marriage? To me it is a vital ten percent. It isn't nearly as glamorous, seductive, or powerful as our sex-obsessed culture tells us. It's important but not that important.

There are many things that go into a successful marriage: friendship, companionship, sacrifice, deep understanding, cooperation, common goals and values, commitment and spiritual unity. Without these things, the physical aspects of a relationship are relatively shallow and meaningless.

You say a vital ten percent. What do you mean by "vital?" Love-making is a powerful symbol of love and trust. The couple gives to one another in the most intimate way. This is their private world. This is a way to give one another pleasure they can get from no other source. Without the regular closeness of physical intimacy and touch, there is the likelihood for dissatisfaction, hurt, rejection and loss.

Occasionally I've seen couples in a counseling setting who have mutually agreed that physical intimacy isn't important in their relationship. If it isn't an issue for them, it isn't an issue. They are making do with the other 90 percent, which can be wonderful in its own right. More likely though, one partner is concerned or upset by the lack of intimacy in their relationship.

I suppose the next question ought to be, what do you mean "regular?" Without being doctrinaire, I've found that most men and women are quite content with love-making once or twice a week. National surveys suggest, on average, that is what happens between married couples. Men may fantasize and talk like it could or should be more, but when asked the question in therapy, their expectations are remarkably similar to their wives' expectations.

"On average" doesn't mean a programmed schedule, but over time it works out to a predictable frequency. Relationships get in trouble when too much time passes between this vital connection. Anything over a month to six weeks between love-making has the potential for harming the relationship. If a couple goes longer than two or three months without intimacy, it creates distance between them.

Why does this happen? Why does sex drop out of their relationship? Love-making is a sensitive barometer of other problems in their relationship. Emotionally, it is difficult to be vulnerable, open and giving sexually when there are unresolved problems. Other things have to be right for physical intimacy to be natural. Anger gets in the way when there hasn't been a reconciliation or forgiveness.

Oftentimes the way to restore intimacy is by working hard to resolve hurts and problems. Couples need to get along, give acceptance, accommodate one another, be friendly, love each other freely and nourish their marriage. If feelings are positive, loving and supportive, a willingness to be physically close to each other is created.

Can the fight be about sex, pure and simple? It can be. Typically, but not always, it is husbands who are more sexually motivated and make overtures that are perceived as inappropriate in terms of mood, timing and privacy. They are "all hands." "Innocent" touch becomes progressively more sexual and demanding.

Right or wrong, his partner perceives the goal to be love-making. To short circuit the process, she adopts a chilly, cold reaction to his touch. He interprets this as rejection and is offended by her lack of warmth and receptivity. In bed and at other times, she would welcome some nonsexual holding and cuddling, but believing that it can't be left at that, she pulls away.

This battle isn't about love-making - it is about poor communication and lack of restraint. I recommend that couples practice non-sexual touch to get close so that touching doesn't mushroom into conflict about sex.

In the scenario just described, what is the answer to break up this cycle? Less is more. Keep physical affection clearly non-sexual. If it has a sexual tinge to it, be certain that it isn't progressive. Have clear boundaries and read each other's signals well. Men need to learn to set the stage for infrequent, but meaningful, mutually rewarding love-making. This means paying attention to mood, unresolved conflict, fatigue, and privacy concerns.

No means "not now." It doesn't mean rejection. Also, women who feel rejected in their overtures to love-making feel equally hurt, upset and angry.

It may be a cliche, but husbands need to understand that women aren't as directly "wired' for sexual arousal as men. Emotional and physical foreplay are essential. Other aspects of the relationship are important - feeling loved, cared for, appreciated, respected, listened to, understood, and taken seriously. An occasional romantic surprise can be special.

What are the most frequent complaints men have? They would like their wives to periodically take the initiative in love-making. It means something to the male psyche to be sought after and desired. If a wife would do this every fifth time, it would seem like 50 percent to her husband.

A second complaint has to do with the range of sexual expression. The bottom line is the relationship has to be mutually pleasurable. Some behaviors can't be negotiated. Some can. That is just the way it is. Open, sensitive discussion will clear up any misunderstandings.

WOMEN, SEX *IS* IMPORTANT
CHAPTER THIRTY

How do men feel about sex? For all you ever want to know on the subject, just purview the women's magazines at your local grocery store. It is a staple feature. I suppose the pornography magazines have something to say about it, too, but not of the healthy variety.

I have had the added benefit of trying to help many couples resolve their sexual difficulties in marriage. Some common themes pop up from the male perspective on common complaints about sexual problems in their marriages.

1. Sexual fulfillment is an important emotional need in marriage. Many men list sexual fulfillment as one of their top three emotional needs - quite accurately predicted by their spouses.

An interesting difference between men and women is that when a man's top three or four needs are met in the relationship, he is generally content and doesn't get too disturbed when other needs are not met. Women, on the other hand, expect a much larger range of needs met in order to be content in their marriage. Not often do they list sexual fulfillment as one of their top three needs. Emotional intimacy and affection are frequently mentioned.

The conventional wisdom on love-making is that men give emotional intimacy and other loving acts in marriage in order to get sex, while women give sex in order to get emotional intimacy and relational connection. For husbands, speaking generally, being loved sexually means being loved. If there is a pattern of a lack of willingness to engage sexually, this magnifies into major hurt and rejection.

Sex can't be subtracted unilaterally from marriage without the husband becoming unhappy. It is especially galling for a husband to believe that his wife fraudulently misled him during courtship and early marriage to believe she enjoyed sex. To him, it now seems like a ploy and as soon as he was safely committed, she flipped an off switch on her sexual desire. His memory of the sensual connection of their early love-making and her current distaste or apathy causes anger and resentment.

A husband laments, *"Sex was supposed to be a part of the marriage bargain, wasn't it? After repeating vows (to have and to hold), everything changes. 'To have' becomes 'to have' when I feel like it and to 'hold off' when I feel like it.'"*

When there are relationship problems such as marital fighting, anger, mis-communication, or busy and demanding lives, the willingness to be physically intimate usually suffers. Husbands don't like that. It adds incentive to both partners to resolve difficulties so their love-making connection doesn't suffer. Men don't like it when their wives use withholding sex as a weapon to manipulate their marriage.

2. Men like sex to be sensual, earthy, visual, spontaneous, frequent, and with abandonment. And don't forget variety. That is a tall order and doesn't always fit with a female's desires, which runs counter to her relational framework for love-making or the reality of her life.

A man would like honest communication and negotiation about the quality and quantity of their sexual relationship instead of his wife arbitrarily controlling how sex happens - or doesn't happen. A man wrote, *"I'd like to think that marriage is a two way street where both people give in, not just the men."*

Another one states, *"Anytime I tried discussing sex with my wife, the response was, 'All you are interested in is sex,' and that was the end of discussion. I don't recall that my wife ever responded much to words, hugs, tender touches, cards, gifts, expressions of endearment, romantic surprises or countless courtesies. I usually just wound up with a stronger feeling of rejection."*

Husbands like it when a wife takes the initiative, acts seductively and flirtatious, and obviously shows her enjoyment. Satisfying a male need in a perfunctory and regimented manner, without feeling or enjoyment, leaves a husband feeling cold and unloved. Not all sex can be great sex but some sex should be.

3. Not all sexual touch is meant as sexual pressure or initiative. Male fascination with female anatomy is part of the biological mystery and design of mating. A pat on the butt is a sign of affection and a kinesthetic reminder of an intimate connection. This is something that husbands and wives can do to each other that others can't. It is a message. It is symbolic of a couple's love and closeness, whether it is in public or private.

Wives can learn to accept this kind of touch without rejection or anger. They can also give this kind of intimate touch - which husbands would love. Sexual touch is not all about sexual pressure, groping or pestering. This kind of touch can be welcomed under certain circumstances.

Sexual touch can be affectionate. A man writes, *"I haven't groped for a long time. When I touch my wife, anywhere, it is with concern about how she may feel about it, whether it's an erogenous area or other (area)."* Part of touch in marriage can be playful, light-hearted and bonding. Husbands like it.

Wives, ask your husbands to read this chapter and ask, "What in here is true for you?"

MEN, WHEN IT COMES TO SEX, LESS CAN MEAN MORE
CHAPTER THIRTY-ONE

Here is a common marital complaint I encounter in my counseling practice. "My husband misinterprets my hugs and caresses as an immediate invitation to the bedroom. I deliberately withhold my affection and loving warmth from him to protect myself. It's not what I want, but I don't know what else to do."

"At other times he is 'all hands.' He tries to fondle me while I'm busy in the kitchen or wherever. If I allow any degree of intimacy, he gets turned on and expects more than I want or am in the mood to give. He has no sense of timing nor awareness of what I'm doing or how I'm feeling."

"I fight off his advances and he thinks I'm rejecting him. He's hurt, angry and frustrated. We don't communicate well on the subject. Gradually I see he is pulling away from me. How do I get through to him that it doesn't need to be this way?"

Sex is a relationship barometer. Sexual activity is a sensitive barometer of how well things are going in the relationship. Marriage needs a dynamic, vital, mutually satisfying sexual life to be really happy.

The frequency of lovemaking a couple finds mutually agreeable should be reliable. Generally if the frequency is less than every three weeks to a month, then problems develop. On average, married couples make love on the order of once or twice a week.

If you're not getting along, are too angry or too indifferent to one another, then lovemaking becomes difficult and falls off. It is a sign that the relationship needs work.

Sometimes there are physical reasons for inadequate arousal or sexual dysfunction. These problems should be discussed with a medical doctor.

The difference between sexual fulfillment and affection. The advice I give to men is to pay attention to the total relationship. Daily love makes a difference. Sexual fulfillment and affection are different needs.

Affection is the expression of love and care through words, hugs, tender touches, cards, gifts, expressions of endearment, romantic surprises and countless courtesies. These expressions communicate interest, the value of the relationship, and concern for a partner's well-being. Showing affection is another way of saying, "I am crazy about you."

Being loving, considerate, thoughtful, kind, helpful and giving has more to do with female sexuality than trying to arouse her physically. These are habits that can be learned.

Ask what your spouse wants in the way of affection and find out what to avoid. If she knows you know what she wants and you don't do it, it will be taken as a sign you don't care. Her "wiring" isn't as direct as a male mistakenly thinks or hopes it is. Respect her mood, energy level, worries, schedule, and need for privacy.

Feeling loved and cherished on a daily basis make a big difference. What happens before the bedroom door closes is what counts. It's a big turnoff to a woman if her husband expects to make love despite what has happened that day or evening.

A friend of mine made these observations about intimate relationships. *"From my point of view, and when talking to other women, many agree that men don't seem to understand our feelings. For them, anytime is a good time. It doesn't matter if we've just had a fight, are ill, tired or whatever.*

"After a few years, foreplay - which is really necessary for a woman - is not necessary for a man. 'We're married now, so let's just get to the good stuff.' That is a real turn-off. And the, 'Gee, I'm sorry that went so fast,' after the hundredth time, isn't much fun either. After a while a woman gets to feel more like an object or a container for her husband's pleasure. She goes into a 'let's get this over' mode. She

doesn't feel loved anymore. And she doesn't want to do it anymore. The French have a saying, 'There is no such thing as a frigid women, only an inept man,' and boy is that true!"

Declaring love-making off limits. Some males feel that if they aren't continually pressuring their wives, they won't have any sexual intimacy at all. Their logic is that this is the time they might get lucky so it is worth the hassle or the rejection.

They don't realize what a turnoff their pressure is. Their wives feel like sexual objects rather than human beings with rights and feelings. When a woman says she doesn't like something (being pestered by unwanted sexual touch, groping), take her at her word. Repeating the intrusive behavior also tells her that you don't care.

If men could back off and allow sexual relations to occur naturally and in concert with their wife's mood and interest, intercourse would occur more often.

With trust that lovemaking will happen on a fairly predictable basis, advances aren't necessary. By understanding when and under what circumstances are appropriate, constant "hustle" can be dropped out of the relationship.

It is helpful and quite powerful when the woman occasionally takes the initiative and communicates her interest. To turn things around, I suggest limiting intercourse to once a week. The wife is committed to seeing it happen. She is given control over the timing and circumstances either through her receptivity or initiative.

Sexual holiday. This is the key. The rest of the time is a guaranteed sexual holiday where flirting, hugs, kisses, hand-holding, touches, caresses, back rubs, etc. are enjoyed for their own sake. Sexual foreplay is not affection. There should be clear communication between an affectionate gesture and a sexual overture. Don't blur the two and the amount of affection will jump astronomically.

A couple can enjoy affection without tension of pushing for or parrying lovemaking. A woman can turn on her warmth and friendliness and receive the non-sexual affection that is important to her. It doesn't take men long to figure out that the friendliness, love and warmth are well worth the restraint they show.

The emphasis on non-sexual affection and playfulness adds to the total relationship and creates a loving marriage - and in the long run, a better and a more loving sexual relationship.

Part VII: Effective Listening and Communication

I see communication as a huge umbrella that covers and affects all that goes on between human beings. Once a human being has arrived on earth, communication is the largest single factor determining what kinds of relationships he makes with others and what happens to him in the world about him. How he manages his survival, how he develops intimacy, how productive he is, how he makes sense, how he connects with his own divinity - all are largely dependent on his communication skills.
- Virginia Satir, Peoplemaking

WANT A GOOD MARRIAGE? HAVE GOOD MANNERS
CHAPTER THIRTY-TWO

What do you think makes the difference between couples who are struggling in their marriages and couples who are not?

A. The effort they put into meeting each other's needs.

B. The frequent expression of appreciation and admiration for each other's positive qualities.

C. The use of respectful communication skills in resolving differences.

The correct answer is "C." Both distressed and non-distressed couples are good at accentuating the positive in their marriages. They meet each other's needs. They are loving, generous and giving. However, distressed couples engage in more destructive communication than non-distressed couples. They perceive their partner in a negative light more of the time.

Unaware of rudeness. The spouses in distressed marriages mean well but what they intend and what comes across are two different things. They are being rude without knowing it. They think they are saying their true feelings and don't take into consideration how hurtful they are being.

They are so anxious to make their points that they don't project a feeling of concern and appreciation for their partner's feelings or point of view. In short, they are poor listeners.

Distressed couples react to each other's moods. They have a hard time being loving and empathic when their partner is out of sorts or out of line. They are quick to join the battle, escalate a quarrel and reciprocate in kind. They have a low tolerance for contrary opinions. Perceived insults do not pass without comebacks.

Their partner, when confronted with a counter argument or "attack," is equally adept and willing to engage in argument, quarreling with details or putdowns. These couples mistakenly feel they can use logic to prevail in an argument. Unfortunately, in an atmosphere of anger and defensiveness, their logic isn't being heard.

They, in turn, do not listen to their partner's logic. Their mind is racing, triggered by the general notion of what is being said. "Yes" is followed so quickly by a "but" that it is obvious that little listening has taken place.

No problem solving. They spin their wheels. They bring up the past. They throw in the kitchen sink. They change the subject. They are easily derailed. Nothing gets solved.

Distressed couples do a lot of mind-reading. They think they know how their partner thinks and feels despite their partner's protests to the contrary. They make their points in excruciating detail and go on and on and on. They dismiss arguments out of hand. "That's not true." They use extreme examples, "you always" and "you never." This invites their partner to take offense or cite an exception.

Distressed couples use sarcasm. They walk off. They ignore. They hold grudges. They give the silent treatment. Even if their words don't communicate disrespect, their body language does.

At a "Smart Marriage, Happy Families" conference, Jack Rosenblum, EdD, JD, of Deerfield, Massachusetts presented a quick reminder to help couples practice good communication habits. He calls it HEART.

"H" stands for "hear and understand me." Couples listen well when they show they care through interest, curiosity and a caring heart. Body language and tone of voice that indicate attentiveness, concern and interest help. Respect his or her right to have the floor in a conversation and draw your partner out so he or she feels completely understood. Don't interrupt. Summarize your partner's point of view before responding. Validate his or her point of view whenever you can honestly do so.

"E" stands for "even if I am 'wrong,' don't make me wrong." Couples can disagree without attacking the personality or showing disrespect to their partner. Don't use sarcasm, blame or find fault. If your partner doesn't feel he or she is at fault, your personal attack will seem doubly wrong and will likely cause an angry reaction. Make the experience of discussing mistakes as pleasant as you can without it becoming an ordeal.

"A" stands for "appreciate the greatness within me." Abundant appreciation and recognition put the total relationship in a positive context. Be grateful and acknowledge the good your partner does and how special he or she really is.

"R" stands for "recognize my positive intent." Most people aren't intentionally trying to inflict harm or hurt. Give your partner the benefit of the doubt. Don't question their motives or commitment to change. Don't tell them what they "really" think or feel. Don't overreact to offensive or provocative statements or quibble with "untrue" details. Stay with the intent of their message.

"T" stands for "tell me the truth with compassion." Be sensitive to your partner's moods, needs and responsibilities before confronting a serious topic. State your own positive intent to find a mutually satisfying solution before launching into a conflict discussion. Be tactful and tentative in the way you talk about something that might affect his or her feelings. Soften your tone of voice.

Shorten up your comments to match the concentration level or listening span of your partner. Be sensitive to their need to disengage and process emotional information before pushing for a solution. Be tentative in your conclusions. Qualify your responses as your opinion only.

If you communicate from the HEART, you will be showing kindness by the mannerly way you give respect and consideration. In distressed marriages, this kindness doesn't come through.

Want a good marriage? Use good manners. Good conversational and listening manners.

How Poor Marital Communication Contributes To Divorce
Chapter Thirty-Three

There are negative patterns of communication that predict divorce. Psychologist John Gottman heads a Marriage Lab research program at the University of Washington. He highlights six of these factors.

1. Too much conflict. If there are too many negative interactions as compared to the number of positive interactions divorce is near. Examples of negative interactions would include harsh judgments, rudeness, criticisms, temper outbursts, blame, hostility and other types of unresolved conflict. Low levels of conflict are a sign of marital health.

Unhappy couples react to their partner's negative emotions - anger, irritability, fear, sadness, blame, defensiveness, whining - with negative emotions of their own. They have high levels of negative emotions and low levels of positive emotions. They try to fix problems with negative emotions or only pay attention to the negative emotions of their partner.

2. Destructive communication. Gottman has identified four destructive communication patterns.

- **Criticism:** finding his or her partner defective, attacking the personality or character of the partner and not focusing on behavior.

- **Defensiveness:** being right, denying responsibility, making excuses, cross complaining, playing the innocent victim, making counter complaints, whining, justifying mistakes and not really paying attention to the message of the partner.

- **Contempt:** insulting or psychologically abusing the partner, communicating superiority by name calling, hostile humor and sarcasm, mockery and body language such as rolling the eyes, sneering, and curling the upper lip.

- **Stonewalling:** a habitual tendency to withdraw physically or emotionally, avoiding, refusing to engage the partner in problem solving, ignoring, or responding with stony silence.

3. Negative emotional arousal. A harsh start up to conflict triggers physiological and emotional arousal in a partner. This, in turn, activates either withdrawal or negative reactions that escalate the conflict. The intensity of the approach defeats the purpose of problem solving.

A typical pattern is that of men either fleeing or attacking under conditions of arousal, while women underestimate the impact of their own emotions on communication problems. It can work both ways however, with some men being emotionally charged and their spouses withdrawing or escalating their own reactions.

4. Failure to repair. Happily married couples sense when arguments are becoming destructive and counterproductive. They make conciliatory gestures such as commenting on the interaction that is taking place, reaffirming love or admiration, keeping the discussion on the subject, soothing, calling time outs, ignoring provocative comments, and using humor to diffuse tension.

They short-circuit negativity and initiate repair attempts by developing what he calls a "positive sentiment override." It is the opposite of having a chip on your shoulder. Negative conflict is interrupted by a desire to put the well being of the relationship ahead of one's own interests or hurts.

Dysfunctional couples escalate conflict while happy couples control the negativity by de-escalating conflict or being quick to repair any damage done in the interaction.

5. Failure to accept the influence of a wife. One of Gottman's more provocative findings is that marriages suffer when men fail to accept the influence of their wives. In other words, if men would just give in and do what women want, then they would set the stage for their own needs being met.

When men fail to pay attention, do not treat their partner as an equal, or fail to engage in a true negotiating process, a pattern of anger and disengagement results. In other words, men need to take their wives seriously instead of giving them lip service or being controlling.

6. Mismatch in styles of conflict resolution. Marital problems occur when there are mismatched styles of conflict resolution. Each partner's style frustrates the other.

Men react to their wives' high or low levels of negative emotion with strong rejection and negative emotions of their own - belligerence, defensiveness or contempt. They either withdraw or escalate the fight. Women take this as rejection.

A husband needs to learn to respond with respect and courtesy when his wife is raising issues or is showing negative emotion. It takes a lot of emotional skill and regulation to ask questions, stay responsive and engaged, show understanding and validate his partner's negative emotions.

Women would be better at conflict resolution if they approached problem-solving with a "soft start up," engaging in respectful persuasion with neutral emotion. Dampening down her own negative emotions and intensity makes it easier for her partner to "hear" her message.

Gottman's main advice is for couples to introduce more positive interactions into the marriage. He suggests doing it in non-conflict situations. It's like depositing money in the bank. At the same time, a couple needs to cut down on negativity during conflict while introducing more positive interactions.

When couples disagree, solving the problem is not as important as controlling the conflict. Every relationship has unsolvable problems. The emotions and gridlock around unsolvable problems discourage and alienate couples. Marriage partners need to learn to regulate their own emotions during conflict.

Gottman also believes couples need to manage their stress so that it doesn't spill over into the marriage. Both need to be adept at buffering or insulating their relationship from outside pressures.

Happy couples can strengthen their friendship and love by sharing emotional intimacy, expressing fondness and admiration for each other, giving undivided attention, being mindful of each other and by being inviting and approachable. Gottman calls this "turning toward" versus "turning away."

Happy couples honor each other's dreams. Listen to each other's dreams more deeply and work to help make those dreams come true. They create a private world of shared meanings, traditions and rituals.

SETTING THE STAGE FOR CHANGE
CHAPTER THIRTY-FOUR

Some couples come into my office like a bull in a china shop. No, I don't sell china nor am I breakable. In fact, when they talk to me, they are polite and respectful. But when they talk to their partner they paw the ground, give withering looks and start to butt heads. In order to survive, their partners attempt to stand their ground and butt back.

Most people are well-meaning and good-hearted. They don't mean to cause all the hurt they inflict, but their communications are blunt and brash. They flare up at a challenge. They fight for territory. There is no finesse, no search for middle ground. They are rude and don't know it.

Little effort is used to understand their mate's point of view. Comments are met with incredulity and defensiveness. Emotional arousal is intense. They can't resist the impulse to interrupt, refute or counterattack.

How do people get to be so fast and loose with their tongues? Don't they realize they are dealing with something fragile and precious? Why don't they pay attention to how words can wound?

No one is listening. Worse yet, if the words and meaning get through, their partner may disregard the emotions behind what they are saying. It is as if the hurt, fear, anger, sadness, worry and confusion don't matter. Instead of warmth, there is hostility. Instead of acceptance, there is rejection. Instead of concern, there is indifference. Instead of patience, there is raw anger. Instead of respect, there is disdain. Instead of charity, there is blame.

There is no varnish on the criticism - no benefit of doubt, no allowance for weakness and no measuring of words. Accusations fall like sledgehammer blows upon the self-esteem of their partner. I don't see much love.

They icily lay out the perceived problem. If the actual words aren't cutting enough, they express harshness through body language and tone of voice. Unspoken communication says a lot more than the actual words being uttered.

One or both may regard counseling as a chance to impress a third party of their righteous cause and to win the battle of who is right and wrong. They do not see counseling as a chance for constructive dialogue with their partner.

Rigidity and criticism. When couples see each other only in a negative light, it interferes with their ability to be empathic and to understand the feelings of the other. A steady exposure to this lack of listening will lead to the conclusion that their partners don't care.

The partner on the receiving end of this treatment gets exasperated. He or she falls into the same style of angry, defensive, and argumentative communication - trying to break through and get understanding.

Endless debates. It doesn't work. This is exactly the kind of dialogue the spouse relishes. What we have now are seemingly endless and repeated arguments that don't get resolved. One common outcome is one partner shuts down and withdraws to avoid the unpleasant confrontations.

When important needs are not being met, one common tactic is to be unpleasant as a means of forcing or coercing change from a partner. Husbands and wives react to each other with anger and/or deny each other pleasure and intimacy in hopes their partner will respond with love and warmth.

It doesn't work, either. Unfortunately, each partner sees the other as withholding love. They are waiting for the 'quid pro quo,' an attitude of "I will do this if you will do that." The problem is that the initial positive action doesn't happen and nobody is being constructive.

The couple may have many things in common - goals, values, religion, love of children, interests, sexual compatibility and a strong commitment to marriage and family life, but the day-to-day negative interactions take a toll. The lack of emotional intimacy and mutual support plus the perpetual conflict create loneliness and isolation. The marriage is being nit-picked to death. Everywhere there are mountains. There are no molehills.

Often, I find my job as a marriage counselor is to help people realize that the world of relationships is a delicate place to be. With a few manners and insights, bulls become as careful and wary as cats entering new territory.

Breaking the impasse. At this point, both partners will have usually withdrawn from actively meeting their partner's needs or are engaged in a power struggle.

Each partner can independently go out of their way for their partner despite whether his or her needs not being met. One partner can initiate changes without his or her mate's awareness or cooperation. It can and does work. When caring changes are introduced, the hostile and rejecting actions of the spouse diminish.

Couples who are that angry with each other may need counseling assistance before they can do this.

Trying at the same time. Miracles can happen when marriage partners see each other trying at the same time. The trick is to get the ball rolling in the first place. Each partner is challenged to act on their own to break up the tit-for-tat mentality that has taken over their marriage.

Act on what you learn. Is it a back rub? Is it a walk? Pick out a few things that are easy for you to do. Do them daily and with no strings attached. Plan a few surprises to show your love in unexpected ways. Lighten up the atmosphere.

It is in the awareness of needs and the willingness to meet them that people learn to trust each other's motives and concerns. If needs are met, then differences and misunderstandings don't seem quite as important.

The miracle is this: as couples turn their attention and energy to meeting their partner's needs, the love they send out will touch and heal some of their hurts. By themselves, loving acts may not be enough to solve all the problems - communication skills still have to be learned - but they certainly set the stage for resolving conflict.

The goodwill created by loving acts makes it easier for a mate to entertain some changes the partner would like. When defenses are lowered, it is easier for a spouse to be perceived as a friend instead of an enemy. When important needs are being met, couples begin to identify each other as a source of pleasure once again.

The problem with this approach is that it can't be sustained for very long if a reciprocal benefit is not received. There is a limit on how much can be given without having the scales balanced. It is worth a try. It is definitely better than staying stuck in separate camps waiting for the other person to make the first move.

Trust. Successful communicators take risks in talking about sensitive subjects when there is a backdrop of love, trust and mutual respect. Security in the relationship grows when each partner appreciates the other's abilities, opinions and essential goodness. A spouse who senses this bedrock of commitment and love will dare to bring up sensitive issues because he or she knows that the marriage isn't continually on trial.

Also, the willingness to talk about delicate problems depends on whether the overall tone of the relationship is positive and mutually rewarding. Touchy subjects bring pain, uncertainty and temporary alienation. The key is that both partners know that the alienation is temporary.

Minimize conflict. People often expect their partner to measure up to their ideal view of how they should be and act in marriage. Because of strong differences they are frustrated and exasperated.

They spend a great deal of time and energy trying to change the 10 percent of their partner's personality, values or goals that will never change. Instead, they could be enjoying the 90 percent that created the attraction in the first place.

Instead of giving healthy acceptance and appreciation as a true friend, they dish out anger, judgment and disappointment. Part of getting on track is letting go of misplaced expectations and committing oneself to making the best of what the situation really is. Differences can be interesting and can enrich a marriage.

Some things are likely to change over time, but not in a climate of criticism and rejection. Spouses learn from each other and gradually take on each other's habits and characteristics. Some things will change only with considerable effort and only when the other party is motivated to change for him or herself.

Pick your fights. Couples don't have to agree on everything, only the important things. Being wise is knowing what to overlook.

Some issues mean a lot more to one person in a relationship than the other. To your mate, they may be principles; to you, they are preferences. On some things, you just give in. Do it gracefully. It is not worth the fight. On other issues, your spouse may choose to give in to you because of your strong feelings. What is "true" may not be "right" when you take your partner into account.

Get to the underlying issues. Disagreements may be masking other problems in a marriage. For example, a couple may be fighting about parenting when, in fact, the husband is feeling neglected or ignored in his personal relationship with his wife. The parenting issue is a "safe" and predictable fight; while addressing the real issue involves more honesty and risk.

Put your problems in the hands of a third party. Generally couples have worked hard to try to solve their problems on their own. Despite their best efforts, their attempts at resolving difficulties haven't succeeded. They really need a third party to help them work through some needed changes.

For couples not yet in counseling, make an appointment and put your problems on hold until you get to the session. Anxiety to resolve problems before things get worse actually makes them worse as destructive patterns are repeated.

For couples with a history of not being able to resolve conflict, I advise them not to work on their problems at home. I want to be present for their discussions on their "hot button" issues. I don't want the couple to get into further arguments between sessions and become even more discouraged. Of course, the goal of therapy is to help the couple gain the skills necessary to solve problems on their own.

With hope, you can keep the peace. The minimum atmosphere I want is one of keeping the peace - being pleasant or neutral. They are encouraged to make small talk about matters that have no bearing on their marital problems.

With the hope that their serious problems will eventually be addressed in counseling, one, if not both partners, welcomes a break from the pressure of needing to do something immediately to break the destructive impasse.

One partner in particular may have been feeling pressure from the other to change. To him or her, a vacation from the problem and from the partner's anxious and unrelenting concern is pleasant relief. If people have hope that their real concerns will be addressed in a safe setting, they can usually put their "hot" topics to the back burner where they can simmer until they are ready to be addressed in counseling.

GROUND RULES FOR COMMUNICATION
CHAPTER THIRTY-FIVE

One of the chief problems in clear communication is the all too human tendency to react and not listen. Too many times marriages become unhappy because of a history of failed attempts to communicate or solve problems.

Our minds are quick. We can comprehend much faster than a

speaker can verbalize. Our minds jump ahead. We anticipate the rest of our partner's thoughts. We stop listening. We formulate our own response. We get impatient. We interrupt. We give our response.

The speaker gets distracted or frustrated. He or she doesn't feel "heard" and redoubles the effort to make his or her point. Or the speaker may feel compelled to respond to what was just said rather than completing his or her original line of thinking. The interchange degenerates into both parties trying to make their points at the same time. They are talking over each other without really listening to the other person's point of view.

Worse yet, the "listener" is easily aroused by the provocative nature of what is being said and impatiently or angrily tries to dispute the other's point of view. This defensiveness and combative posture turn a discussion into an argument with each speaker feeling that his or her opinions are not understood or valued.

All those reactions make the conversation worse. Most likely, the speaker will attempt to get through and probably in a less kindly way.

Without a track record for solving problems together, conversations feel like ordeals that are repeated over and over again. Eventually one party senses the futility of even trying, becomes frustrated or discouraged and withdraws - leaving many important problems unresolved.

Relationships go both ways. People have a responsibility to help the other person understand their feelings. Problems won't be solved unless they are put on the table. Many people regret the way they've handled relationships - they didn't speak up soon enough or didn't persist in getting the point across.

Here are some guidelines for communicating effectively.

- Control your emotions. The number one problem to good listening under these circumstances is your emotional arousal. You don't think as well as you can normally. It is hard to listen when you are upset or aroused. Responding with anger or hostility only makes things worse.

If you are too upset to listen, ask for a break to calm down and try again later. It is important to get back to the conversation in a reasonable length of time and not "use" your arousal to avoid the issue.

- State your positive intent on wanting to understand and resolve the difficulty. You can establish goodwill by affirming your love and concern for your partner and your willingness to try to understand his or her point of view. Express the hope and belief that you can overcome the barriers to communication. Give genuine appreciation and recognition for your spouse's positive qualities and willingness to work on this with you.

When the speaker prefaces their remarks with something like, "I care about you. I know I am upset right now. I want to clear the air so we can enjoy each other again," the attitude of the listener might improve considerably.

- Seek understanding first. The object of communication is not to win the battle of "Who is right?" but to learn to understand and respond to the partner's feelings.

Some people listen for understanding; others listen to rebut or attack. There is a huge difference in attitude. Debaters aren't trying to learn; they are trying to win.

A good relationship depends on minimizing conflict by using tact and judgment in deciding which problems to confront. Knowing how and when to confront a problem is truly a delicate matter.

When problems occur in a relationship, a person needs to give his or her partner the benefit of the doubt. Even something that seems like betrayal or disloyalty may be the result of a misunderstanding.

A gentle spouse refrains from judging the motives of a partner as malicious or self-serving and listens to the other side of the story. When confronted by mistakes or misunderstandings, ask questions and be curious about your partner's thoughts and feelings.

The complaint may be unwarranted, misguided or even meant to hurt. But the mere fact that your spouse said it or believes it makes it important to understand the complaint thoroughly. If there is validity to it, and chances are there is a core of truth to his or her perception, your partner is offering you an opportunity to discuss or correct the problem. One of the blessings of marriage is to have a loving critic, someone who knows you and is willing to share constructive feedback.

- One person has the floor at a time. The person who has the floor has the right to be listened to without interruption. He or she needs to complete thoughts and express feelings with a good listener who is trying to understand.

A speaker is often confronted with a listener jumping in and interrupting with his or her thoughts, opinions, advice, counter-arguments or pearls of wisdom. The speaker doesn't know whether to listen respectfully and respond to what was just said or to persist in an effort to be heard. The speaker doesn't feel listened to and feels frustrated.

- **Use conversational etiquette in passing the floor.** Communication suffers when one party avoids expressing thoughts or feelings or when the other party is too dominant and aggressive in conversations. "Passing the floor" in a conversation equalizes opportunities for communication, especially for correcting problems when one partner may not be assertive enough to really be heard.

The floor can be requested or offered. The listener can inquire if the speaker wants to say anything more about the topic under discussion. The person who has the floor can keep the floor or yield it when requested.

When the speaker relinquishes the floor, he or she shifts into the listening role. The floor can be passed temporarily for a brief clarification or commentary then given back to the speaker to continue.

With no permission to respond, the listener's power of concentration is totally focused on the understanding the message of the speaker. Without competition from his or her own thoughts or personal agenda, a listener can process what is being said. It is easier to listen when there is no intention to respond with intelligent, witty or critical remarks. Paraphrasing accurately will help your partner feel understood and consequently be a better listener for you.

When the listener's anxiety, anger, sorrow or arousal level is too great, he or she needs to be the speaker. Recognizing and responding to these emotional cues is an important key on when to pass the floor. Trading the floor back and forth helps a couple go deeper into each side of the disagreement and develop empathy and compassion for each other.

- **Agree to discuss one problem at a time.** The topic under discussion will touch on other potential issues and problems. Don't get bogged down by trying to deal with several issues at once. Make a mental note to bring up the new issue in a separate discussion. Keep focused on the issue at hand.

- **Stay in the present**. By bringing up provocative hurts and unfinished business from the past, there is a good chance the conversation will be derailed. Instances from the past shouldn't be brought up unless they are clear examples of how the current problem is part of an ongoing pattern. Even at that, concentrate on the current situation. Don't bring up past problems to get even or to change the subject.

- **Allow time for tensions to decrease.** Each person needs time to think through what has been said. Follow-up sessions on the same topic may be necessary before issues finally take shape. Respect the other's need for time to think about what was said and to regroup if either of you is frustrated or angry.

- **If what is being said is true and you agree with it, apologize.** Many issues won't die because the speaker hasn't felt there has been a sufficient apology. If the complaint involves a current behavior, commit yourself to a course of action or, at a minimum, ask for time to think over what you are willing to do about it. Some conversations won't go away until there is a resolution of the problem.

- **Try to end the conversation on a good note.** Summarize any commitments made or solutions to be carried out. Express respect for the speaker's opinion and the courage it took to share honestly.

- **Practice relationship skills to become good at them.** How couples manage their differences through effective communication and conflict resolution skills is an overwhelming factor in predicting successful relationships. Conversely, destructive communication patterns shown during courtship and early marriage are highly predictive of later difficulties.

Couples can learn and practice agreed on rules for handling strong, negative feelings that are a part of all relationships. They can learn how to handle their "hot thoughts" and "quick tongues."

Couples can practice and apply these skills in low conflict controlled situations and then gradually apply them to major and explosive areas of conflict. These changes need to be practiced until they are automatic responses, even under stressful conditions. People can change if they work at it.

If you can follow this pattern, especially with a loved one who is unhappy with you, you will have done something hard – one of the harder things to do in life. You will also have new skills for self-correcting a relationship and solving problems as you go.

Tell Your Truth With Compassion
Chapter Thirty-Six

Good communicators develop an emotional vocabulary to express their inner feelings and experiences. Describing emotions, talking from the heart, and giving non-judgmental attention to others' feelings promotes connection and unity.

People need to really open up and say their true feelings. With the miracle of dialogue and understanding, bridges can be crossed, hands are extended and genuine caring is shared. If politeness and respect become a part of the language we use, the door is open for genuine communication.

The truth hurts. The truth also heals. The art of communicating is to tell the truth so that it can be understood. The art of communicating is to tell your truth with compassion. But the truth needs to be told. Even the best listeners can't fill in the gap of what is not shared.

Here are some guidelines to help you be effective in getting your thoughts and feelings across.

1. Choose a good time and place. Use good timing when bringing up a topic. Timing is everything. Choose an appropriate time and place when you are prepared and have the energy you need - not when you are overly stressed and overwhelmed.

Choose a location that is comfortable and puts you on your best behavior. Talking over problems after a meal at a restaurant may be a good place. If at home, sit, don't stand.

Be aware of your partner's stress levels and schedule. Try to discuss a distressing topic while it is still current. Discuss sensitive issues in private. Be aware of your partner's readiness to receive the information.

2. Show respect. Use common courtesy. Don't use profanity, yelling, name calling or other forms of derogatory address to make your point. Don't attack the listener's character or personality. Don't try to bring up an issue while you are angry unless you know your partner can handle your emotions and can listen to your anger.

The process of communicating needs to be relatively pleasant, not an ordeal. Speak in a way that preserves your partner's dignity and self-respect.

3. Start slowly and softly. Use a calm tone of voice. Don't overwhelm your partner with strong emotion, especially at the beginning of a difficult discussion. Ease into your discussion by stating your intent to be positive and constructive.

Body language and tone of voice can soften up a conversation. If there is a discrepancy between what you say and how you say it, your non-verbal messages will be believed first. He or she may be reacting to the tone of your voice instead of your words. If you are emotional, acknowledge it.

Minimize defensiveness by starting with what you agree on. Acknowledge their concerns. Recognize at the outset that your partner has a valid point of view and will have ample opportunity to express it.

Express how you feel. Describe the problem and don't judge. Ask them to reflect back to you their understanding of your concerns. Clarify any points they may have misunderstood.

4. Minimize inflammatory or exaggerated statements. Avoid extreme examples or words that could be a distraction from the main point. Choose milder expressions than the ones your partner used. For example, if you hear the words, "you always," or "you never," summarize with "you frequently" or "you seldom" to bypass disputing their choice of words. Ignore factual disputes and summarize the underlying meaning or theme of what he or she is trying to get across.

5. Don't be judgmental. Part of communicating is to speak so the defenses of the other party are reduced. I've seen people state their truth in such an aggressive and abrasive manner that communication breaks down immediately.

Here are some examples of judgmental comments. "That's not true!" "That's not what happened at all!" "I disagree. What it's really all about is . . ." "You're wrong." "I don't know how you could possibly think that." "That's a bunch of B.S.!" "That's dumb. That's really, really dumb. There is no way in hell that..."

Other comments give the impression that you are an authority on what they think or feel. The listener feels there is no way he or she can win. Examples include: "How you really feel is . . ." "You haven't heard a thing I've said." "That's not right! What you meant to say was . . ."

Other comments that shut down communication are those that express outrage, total lack of credibility and dramatic disbelief. Examples include: "I can't believe you said that!" "That couldn't be true! If I thought for a minute that was true, I'd . . ." "What's wrong with you? Don't you remember . . ." "Here we go again. You and your stupid idea that . . ."

6. Don't overload. The speaker needs to become familiar with the attention span of the listener. By using elaborate descriptions, excessive detail or piggybacking too many ideas or issues into a non-stop monologue, many speakers lose their listeners early on and don't know it. Give your opinions in bite-sized chunks so your spouse won't be overloaded.

Too much emotion, anger or powerful ideas strung together can overload the listener. On key comments ask to see if the listener understood the point you were trying to make. If you are not satisfied your spouse has heard you, tactfully ask for a summary of your main points before going further into the conversation.

7. Show openness by using conditional language. By qualifying one's remarks, a tone of respect and openness is communicated. This is done by using tentative language and by acknowledging the validity of another's point of view. Partners can listen to challenging ideas and opinions when they feel there will be a fair exchange.

Here's what I mean by tentative or conditional language: "I may be wrong, but this is how I see it." "It seems to me, and you may feel differently, . . ." "For what's it's worth, here's how I feel." "I'm not sure I'm right, but this is how I see it." "I might be off base, and if I am, please help me understand. At any rate, here's what I think." "This is my opinion, which you may disagree with. . ." "I can see what you are saying about how I add to the problem in this way, but I also feel that what happens then is ..."

These expressions concede that the truth is open to question and there are other points of view. It shows the speaker is open to new information and the points under discussion can be negotiated.

By using this phrasing, the speaker tells the listener that it is truly a two-way communication and that mutual influence can occur. The listener, hearing respectful phrases, relaxes his or her defenses and can really listen to what is being said.

By changing the way opinions are expressed, the legitimacy of another person's opinion is recognized. A judgmental and opinionated person is usually so sure of their position that phrasing their thoughts as an opinion is difficult. The effort required to use these phrases is an education in itself about how rigid and closed one may be.

By using tentative or qualified language, even a strongly opinionated person will learn to respect the perspectives of others. The language we use has the potential for controlling our own attitude toward the listener. That is a lot of power.

8. Be genuine. Describe your feelings in the here-and-now. If speakers learn to communicate in the here-and-now about details of what is going on with themselves, there is little room for dispute. Communicating details of what is going on in any given moment in a way that does not blame anyone promotes connection more quickly than any one communication skill.

Examples of this include:

- *Body sensations.* "Right now I feel like I have butterflies in my stomach." "I was in a fog and drifted off and missed what you just said." "When you apologized, it felt like a big weight had been lifted off my shoulders."

- *Core feelings.* "I am scared to death about what you are about to tell me." "I was too embarrassed by what I did and tried to cover it up."

- *Specific thoughts/imaginings/interpretations.* "When you didn't answer me, I took that as a 'yes'." "I was distracted by my own thoughts and didn't really hear that last point." "I got confused by what I perceived as sarcasm in your voice and didn't know if you really meant what you just said."

- *Familiar patterns and experiences.* "Once I get angry, it takes me a while to want to work on the problem. I generally hold a grudge for a while." "When you get that look in your eye, I shut down and don't even want to try."

9. Tactfully interrupt interruptions. A tactful interruption is done without irritation or blame. Remind your spouse that you have the floor and wish to finish your points. If he or she can no longer listen to you, temporarily yield the floor, but remind your partner of your right to the floor once you become the speaker again.

Once you have the floor again, state your point once more. If there are more interruptions, commit your partner to not interrupting you until you have finished.

10. Be compassionate. Give the benefit of the doubt. Give your partner some wriggle room to save face. Don't challenge his or her excuses and self-justifications head on. When you come back to your point, integrate his or her thoughts and feelings into your description of the problem. If you can find some way of agreeing with part of what your spouse said, he or she will be more inclined to accept your point of view.

11. Be ready to switch to the listener role. If your spouse is defensive, distraught, angry or resistant of what you have to say, temporarily stop trying to make your point. Your partner may not be willing to listen to you until he or she first feels understood.

CRITICISM IN MARRIAGE IS A DELICATE PROPOSITION
CHAPTER THIRTY-SEVEN

In several studies comparing happy and distressed couples, one consistent finding was that happy couples criticized less often. Couples who are angry and hostile are quick to criticize each other. These criticisms are either meant or said in a destructive or hurtful way. Tone of voice, body language, and an assaulting choice of words rip away at the fabric of trust and security in marriage.

Unfortunately, these judgmental comments are not cushioned by words of concern, friendship or interest. The contrast between frequent critical and infrequent supportive comments creates a negative tone in the relationship.

Negative consequences. What happens? Heavy doses of criticism shut down dialogue, arouse defenses, and drain a relationship of its goodwill. Both partners want to be loved and accepted; not held up to their spouse's measuring rod and found inadequate.

Marriage is a relationship where partners expect their mate to be a friend, a person with whom they can share intimate thoughts safely. It is hard to want to be close to someone who is seldom pleased or satisfied with your behavior or personality.

Too much criticism leads to low levels of self-esteem and mutual support. It is a barrier to physical and emotional intimacy. It can be perceived as control or coercion. Criticizing a spouse should be infrequent.

The first and best thing a fighting couple can do is stop the barrage of negative and disrespectful judgments and find loving, sensitive ways to share concerns.

Guidelines on how to give criticism.

- If in doubt, don't. Some faults can be lived with. It isn't fair to expect perfection. Accept some exasperation and frustration as normal. Don't let your desire to change a few annoying habits destroy the positive and solid connection you have between you.

Unless your spouse asks for advice, chances are he or she won't appreciate it when it is given.

- Resist the temptation to take over your partner's problem. When he or she is struggling with weight problems, smoking, problem drinking, or some other behavior that is hard to change, being over-involved and trying to help seems like control. Don't slip into the role of being a helpless cheerleader or an aversive taskmaster.

Ideas of autonomy and self-reliance run deep. Your partner may be stubborn just to prove he is in charge of his own life. Giving advice can backfire even when it is the "right" advice.

- Don't be too quick. If you are unclear about a problem, try to understand it before jumping in and blundering over tender feelings. Hurtful comments made in haste are remembered. Seek to understand by listening to his or her side of the issue before making any judgments.

- Don't avoid issues. Some grievances can't be ignored. There are facts that have to be faced. Reacting with hurt, brooding, and chilly silence can be just as destructive as making cruel comments in the heat of the moment.

Hurt festers in the privacy of one's own thoughts. Sacrifice your pride and clear up misunderstandings before they become magnified by silence and inattention. In some ways withdrawal is more hurtful to a relationship than angry criticism.

- Explore your spouse's side of the issue. Show understanding first. People want to feel that their problem is understood, then they begin to trust the advice they are given.

Even if you understand, people rightly feel they are unique and their situation is unique. Before you will be able to influence your partner, spend time appreciating the unique aspects of his or her problem.

There are two sides to every story. Listen and be open to

influence and correction. What starts out as criticism may end up as a meaningful two-way exchange with your role also examined.

 - **Don't surprise your mate or catch him or her off guard.** Give notice that you want a serious discussion. Timing is crucial. There is a right time, place and mood when your partner will be most receptive. Negotiate an acceptable time.

 - **Don't criticize your spouse in public.** Protect your spouse from any embarrassment. Wait until you are in private to bring up complaints. Public expressions of sarcasm, contempt or other forms of disrespect are humiliating.

 - **State your positive intent.** Reassure your spouse that the discussion you want is an effort to improve your relationship. Don't launch into negative comments without first setting the stage that you are trying to be constructive in your efforts. Put the distressing topic into an overall context of positive interactions.

 - **Non-verbal language speaks loudly.** Be seated. Use a calm, normal tone of voice. If you get angry, you may create anger or withdrawal before you have a chance to make your points. Your body language and tone of voice will communicate your goodwill and be believed more than your words will be.

 - **Be constructive.** Avoid blame. Stick to behavior and issues. Don't make global assessments of your partner's personality or character. Don't threaten or ridicule. Be tactful and diplomatic in the words you choose. Your criticism is not more important than whatever problem you are trying to correct.

Advice is not usually disliked because of what it is but because of the way it is given. Advice needs to be given softly and gently, indirectly – not like a sledgehammer driving home a harsh truth. This is done by stories, anecdotes, examples of people in similar situations, or with humor. The softer style of communicating can get through whereas a frontal assault with unvarnished truth may be too threatening to deal with.

Being too direct or too strong may add to the sense of failure or incompetence the person may be feeling. Acknowledge the difficulty and complexity of their problem. If advice is given, it should be couched in a way that allows the dignity and self-respect of the recipient to remain intact.

 - **Limit your criticism to a single topic or goal.** Focus on a specific problem. Limit your description of the problem to three or four sentences. Stay within your partner's attention span. Be aware of any emotional reaction that may interfere with his or her ability to absorb what you are saying.

- **Help your partner come up with his or her own solution**. Before offering suggestions, ask thought-provoking questions that help your partner think through their dilemma. By asking good questions, he or she can verbalize thoughts, define the problem more clearly and identify his or her own solutions. If it's their solution, they will be more likely to commit and act on it than if the solutions come from someone else.

- **Give your partner time to think about it.** Some people may not think well on their feet. When he or she is ready, listen carefully to the response. Listening is a key. Both of you want to feel understood and cared about. Be prepared to be open to his or her influence and corrective thoughts.

- **Be prepared to be specific.** Be prepared with specific solutions. If you haven't, it may appear you are dumping a problem instead of sharing a commitment to resolve it. Express your commitment to work on the problem and help in whatever way possible.

Come to an agreement and a commitment about a specific solution. The solution has to fit both of your needs.

- **Don't attach strings to your advice.** Your partner needs the freedom to reject advice and still be accepted. Otherwise advice giving can be seen as a form of manipulation or possible rejection. This is hard if a loved one appears to be making repeated mistakes and ignores your advice.

The ultimate test of love and respect is to stand by and be supportive, despite everything. Rejection of advice shouldn't be taken personally. Don't make your partner feel guilty if he or she chooses not to follow your advice.

- **Follow the criticism with an expression of appreciation, love and support.** Harsh words are remembered, sometimes for a lifetime. When advice is given, it should be followed by an expression of love and concern. Even a small laceration needs a huge dressing, lovingly administered.

End on a good note. A closing expression of love and concern is essential to the process. By having the process end constructively, you build trust so that you can raise other concerns later to fine tune your marriage.

- Be patient and allow time for the change to unfold. Accept your partner's efforts to change at face value instead of questioning his or her motives. Be patient and give ample opportunity for change to occur before bringing up the issue again. Express appreciation for the effort being made.

There it is - a formula for success in an area that is almost as delicate as brain surgery.

WATCH YOUR LANGUAGE - YOUR BODY LANGUAGE
CHAPTER THIRTY-EIGHT

What do you believe – words, tone of voice or body language? Research findings show that if there is a discrepancy between the various modes of communication, 7 percent rely on the words, 38 percent rely on the tone of voice, and 55 percent rely on body language. If the three modes of communication are congruent, belief in the content of what you have to say becomes equivalent with belief in body language and tone of voice.

You are like a book. Your eyes, face, and voice are the title page that will invite a reader to delve further into your experience.

Body language. Body language means hand gestures, body posture, openness of the arms, lean of the body, facial expressions, tilt of the head, and other signals. It is a subtle nonverbal language. Learned from infancy along with verbal language, it is a trustworthy guide to meaning.

"Look into the face of the person to whom you are speaking if you wish to know his real sentiments, for he can command his words more easily than his countenance." – Chesterfield

In teaching couples listening skills, I notice their general turning toward or turning away from each other during conflict. I also notice their smile, open posture, eye contact, forward lean of their body, compassionate touch at key moments, space between them, and head nods that show close attention. When there is exceptional rapport, even body movements become synchronous.

Sometimes a particular individual may have mastered the basic skills of listening to the words and even mechanically reflecting the meaning back, but his or her body language communicates disbelief, disinterest and disapproval of what they are hearing.

By expressing one's opinion through negative body language - frowning, rolling eyes in disbelief or contempt, nodding "you're wrong," or giving a bored or indifferent look - a listener can effectively shut down or agitate a speaker.

The eyes, a veritable window to the soul, are another key to communicating. Eyes can show acceptance or rejection, love or hostility, hope or despair, gratitude or indifference, admiration or contempt, threat or safety – the whole gamut of human emotion. Animals know this. If they want to know about human intention, they look at people right in the eyes.

"An eye can threaten like a loaded pistol, or can insult, like a hissing or kicking; or in an altered mood, can, by beams of kindness, make the heart dance with joy." - Emerson

Tone of voice. The meaning of words can be completely altered to its opposite by the tone of voice. The voice is another mirror of the heart. Are the tones we hear soft, gentle, and inviting, or are they shrill, hard, and disapproving? A raised voice betrays anger even before the angry person may be aware of it. We understand attitudes and emotions such as doubt, enthusiasm, discouragement, kindness and fear by the way they are said, not by the words alone.

People can learn to mask their tone of voice as cleverly as a poker player masks facial expression and body language. It isn't easy, however. Comparatively speaking, the spoken word is far easier to disguise. No wonder we scan all three modes of communication and attempt to integrate them into a coherent message before we trust our understanding.

Tone of voice (belligerent, incredulous, defensive, skeptical, mechanical, argumentative, etc.) also communicates powerfully that the listener has a definite opinion about the topic and is disputing or not caring about the speaker's point of view.

In marriage counseling, I coach couples to pay attention to their body language and tone of voice so they are giving clear and unambiguous messages. If they mean to reconcile, their non-verbal language says a lot about how they are feeling about each other. Some people need to be easier to read. They need to project non-verbal language of love and intimacy more than they currently do.

Misinterpretation. If you think words are easily misunderstood, try body language and tone of voice. I see many individuals who believe they hear and know better what another person is feeling or thinking because of their assumptions they are making based on non-verbal messages.

Sometimes they are intuitive and right on the mark, while other times they are dead wrong. Right or wrong, it is dangerous. Body language and tone of voice can be denied, sometimes rightfully so. Arguments about what non-verbal communication really means go nowhere and arouse anger. They can't be resolved through debate as easily as disputes about words.

The perceiver, in order to justify a preferred explanation of what is going on, interprets body language and tone of voice in line with what he or she already believes.

"Eyes will not see when the heart wishes them to be blind. Desire conceals truth, as darkness does the earth." - Seneca

This is a delicate matter. Is the perceiver on to something truthful or is this a provocative insinuation based on a projection of inner need? The way around this is to take the person at their word, trust their spoken intent and look for results in actions that make their words ring true. The speaker deserves the benefit of the doubt.

I have seen spouses driven crazy by their jealous partners reading way too much into their tone of voice, their glances and even their smallest actions. Nothing the innocent spouse can say or do alleviates the fears of his or her insecure mate. On the other hand, an affair is often discovered through the intuitive reading of non-verbal behavior.

When people are making changes, their non-verbal behavior communicates care and concern and matches the changes being made. People need time to observe, trust and experience changes in the non-verbal arena as a part of regaining trust.

Listeners need to summarize in a "caring" way what they are hearing. Caring is best shown non-verbally. When body language and tone of voice match the content of what the listener is summarizing, the speaker relaxes and feels understood. When they don't match, the speaker interprets the non-verbal communication as the true message.

Challenging non-verbal communication. Another big mistake in communication is that people often read more into body language and/or tone of voice than the speaker believes is true.

People don't like being told what they *really* think or feel based on someone's interpretation of non-verbal communication. They are the experts on themselves and want to be believed. An argument about non-verbal communication is an argument nobody wins. There is no right or wrong, except what the speaker says it means.

Instead of assuming you know what discordant non-verbal communication means, ask about it. Listeners can adopt a posture of being mystified by the mismatch, point it out and ask for a clarification. "You seem angry, is that right?" The speaker can focus on his or her feelings and proceed to explain in greater depth what he or she is trying to communicate.

To summarize:

- If you are a listener, use your very best non-verbal listening skills, body posture, facial expressions, focused attention and kind tone of voice.

- If you are a listener and you are getting mixed messages between verbal and non-verbal language, gently inquire about the discrepancy and be prepared to accept the response at face value.

- Do not debate the meaning of a speaker's non-verbal behavior or assume you know better what is really meant.

Non-verbal language is a pathway to intimacy. One frequent complaint in marital relationships is one spouse feels unloved, unappreciated, lonely, and that he or she doesn't really matter to their partner. There are many reasons for this including lack of time and attention to the relationship, lack of affection, lack of recreational companionship, harsh and disrespectful arguments, or a host of other problems.

Many times, it is wives who are frustrated with insufficient emotional response of their husbands. Some men aren't very expressive. Their language of love is service, companionship, financial support or other things they "do" to demonstrate their love.

While they are doing what they think should be adequate, their wives are frustrated by their monotone tone of voice, their factual, matter-of-fact manner, or their jumping to advice giving or problem solving. They don't express their love with emotion in their voice. They are not soft and soothing in the way they reach out to comfort their wives.

Their apologies are not heartfelt and are said without the emotion that shows they really care. They don't show enough enthusiasm in their fun or enough excitement in their greetings. Their non-verbal behavior makes their spouses wonder if they really care. But they do. And they don't like being told they don't. Their lack of emotional responsiveness can be addressed by directly improving their non-verbal communication.

Coaching non-verbal behavior. In marital counseling, I first help men listen compassionately to their wives' emotions. That helps them connect with their own feelings.

In their responses, I help men soften and lower their tone of voice, put emotion in their voices, lean forward, look into the eyes of their partner, hold or stroke their hand and speak from the heart. In some cases I help them articulate their feelings with an emotional vocabulary, one they are not used to using.

They then put their own thoughts into words and proceed to touch their spouses' hearts with their words and feelings that have long been missing between them. Some men need to be shown a second or third time. At home they practice putting emotion into their voice and an attitude of caring into their body language. Communication just doesn't happen with the brain. It happens with the whole body.

THE ART OF LISTENING
CHAPTER THIRTY-NINE

Your spouse has just unloaded on you. It feels bad. It feels like a personal attack. What do you do? Do you counterattack with something you're upset about? Do you get defensive and dispute the criticism? Do you get angry and withdraw in a huff or brooding silence? Do you roll your eyes in contempt and attack the motives of your mate? If you do, you've already primed the conversation for failure.

People have different backgrounds and traditions. Each is amazingly complex and different. If a partner brings up a problem, the first impulse should be to say, "Tell me more about that." Ask for examples. Try to find out why this issue is so important to them.

Draw out his or her past experiences with similar type problems. Finding connections in their family history and background may explain why a person might feel the way he or she does. This will help you connect with deeper understanding without taking the issue too personally. Really understanding your partner's pain may cause you to view him or her with more compassion.

Listening shows an attitude of respect and concern for the validity of their partner's point of view. Far too many people have the habit of interrupting, giving their side of the story and arguing the point incessantly. They do not listen and appreciate what the other person is saying. Once people have been heard and understood, then they can become problem-solvers.

1. Stay in the listener role. Until you get the floor, you are stuck as a listener. Don't give your own opinion or counter-argument to what is being said. Allow your spouse's point of view to be expressed fully and completely. A good listener learns to put his or her opinions and emotions on hold until he or she legitimately gains the floor. Don't smuggle in your own opinions as leading questions.

Hold onto your thoughts and reactions until you have gained the floor. It is surprising how well you can listen when your only role is to listen and understand.

The tone of voice or body language the listener uses may carry messages of disapproval, disbelief, disinterest, or ridicule. Obvious non-verbal signals can show disagreement, impatience, disgust, anger, discouragement or other emotions. Don't resort to non-verbal means to engage in a rebuttal process.

2. Try to "read the feelings" of the speaker. Though not desirable, the speaker can be "as nasty as he or she wants to be." It is up to the listener not to overreact to inaccuracies, provocative expressions, exaggerations or details. The speaker may use an off-putting tone of voice or body language that is disturbing, but the listener stays with the intent of the message. By artful paraphrasing, the listener can deliberately minimize or bypass content that otherwise could be disputed.

Stick to the main point the speaker is trying to make and don't quarrel with the way he or she tried to make it. Listeners need to be aware of the speaker's body language and tone of voice to understand what is being said.

3. Summarize key points in a caring manner. Your only role is to listen, reflect back what you are hearing, ask relevant or clarifying questions and try to understand the speaker's point of view. Summarize or paraphrase key points to verify with the speaker that true understanding is taking place.

Leave your own side out of the discussion for the time being. If you aren't trying to respond, this frees up your mind to be a better listener. Immediate retorts, interruptions, canned answers and even thoughtful explanations will make your partner wonder if you understood his or her point. An accurate summary shows you've actually heard what was being said.

Check out your listening with an "Is that right?" to give your partner a chance to correct your understanding or to emphasize a point. Help bring feelings into the open. Listen for understanding, not for the purpose of winning an argument. Learn to detach from your thoughts and feelings while you concentrate on what your partner is saying.

Listen with your heart. Describe the issue from the other person's point of view. Try to imagine how you would feel if you were in his or her situation. Listen to anger without reacting. Help your partner save face by ignoring or minimizing clearly offensive behavior.

Don't overreact to the way things are said and don't quibble over details. Go with the intent and feeling. Ignore any communication habits that may be distracting. The summary should minimize or soften provocative or exaggerated language into milder vocabulary. Listen for areas of agreement.

Showing understanding doesn't mean the listener agrees with the speaker. It does mean that the listener is patiently waiting his or her turn to be the speaker. Some listeners like to make brief notes as a reminder of points they might want to react to later.

4 Ask open-ended questions. The listener needs to adopt a curious attitude about what the speaker is saying and gently probe for further details and explanations. By being a sounding board and asking good questions, the speaker can use the listener's feedback as a springboard to deeper background and share emotional experiences connected to their opinions.

One dangerous use of listening is when the listener tries to shape the speaker's thinking by asking leading questions. Asking leading questions is a way of smuggling in one's own thoughts through distorted summaries of what the speaker said.

5. Let your partner wind down, especially if he or she has a lot of emotion. Ask if he or she has anything more to say. "Is there anything else you would like to add?"

6. Watch your body language and tone of voice. With body language, you have to be aware of your smile, open posture, forward lean of your body, touch when appropriate, eye contact and space which is optimal at 2 to 4 feet. As a listener, make sure your facial expression, posture, tone of voice and body language isn't expressing an attitude of disbelief, contempt or disinterest while you are "mouthing" the correct words. Don't be mechanical or technical.

An attitude of caring and empathy is just as important as the skill you show in the actual listening process.

7. Interrupt. It is OK to interrupt when you are being overloaded with too much information. You can teach the speaker about your attention span. You can also let the speaker know when you are being flooded with anger or sorrow or other arousing emotions which interfere with your ability to listen. You can interrupt for clarification also.

None of this is easy to do. Stick to the ground rules and you'll have the best chance of working out your differences.

TAKING CRITICISM WITHOUT BEING DEFENSIVE
CHAPTER FORTY

D o you know anyone with paper thin skin? Is it your spouse - or is it you? Taking criticism is hard because it requires a most difficult skill - the ability to control one's emotions and thoughts while listening and understanding what the critic is saying.

Failure to take criticism causes a breakdown in the communication and problem-solving process. It is frustrating for the other party who feels they are raising a legitimate issue in a constructive way and hoping for a dialogue. Instead, what he or she gets is an argument, a counter-attack, anger, defensiveness or emotional withdrawal and disengagement.

The best way to take criticism is to be a good listener and really care about the intent and message being given. Many of the following suggestions are summarizing key points in the previous chapter, "The Art of Listening."

Emotional control. Arousal caused by criticism interferes with the ability to listen. The "threatened" individual is flooded with emotion or thoughts that interfere with listening carefully to what is being said. His or her reaction is based on faulty assumptions and the response is off the mark. The discussion goes nowhere.

I teach listening skills as part of my couple's counseling. I get an immediate read on how difficult the communication problems are to correct by the listener's ability to detach, understand and empathize with the other person's point of view.

Even if the "criticism" complaint or issue being brought up is seen as unreasonable, untrue or distorted in some way, can the recipient recognize that the other person's perception is a legitimate concern and needs to be understood? The mere fact that the critic believes it makes it important. It takes emotional control to listen to a differing point of view and hear the person out.

Learning to be patient. Good conversational etiquette requires an awareness of who has the floor, and a willingness to hear and understand the other person's point of view. It is also important to give an adequate summary of the problem being raised before requesting a chance to respond to the issue. The real test of this skill comes when the couple learns to do this under tense and emotional conditions.

Some people mistakenly believe that by being a good listener they are agreeing with the things being said. This is not true. All that is being demonstrated is that they understand what is being said, not that it is being agreed to. Having confidence that the listening role will be reciprocated relaxes the listener so he or she does not interrupt or try to take over until the other party has finished.

Positive intent. However, there is a good chance the criticism is valid or that, at a minimum, there is a kernel of truth to what is being said. The critic obviously cares about the situation and is trying to repair a problem. What is being offered is a chance to learn about oneself and/or the relationship. His or her viewpoint is an important source of feedback about reality. Confronting a problem is an invitation to personal growth and to an improved relationship.

Here is a quick review of "do's" and "don'ts" in dealing with criticism. A well meaning critic is hoping to be heard and understood.

- Control your emotion. Be careful on negative body language, sarcasm or hostile and angry responses. Hurt or brooding silence is not productive. Don't interrupt. Don't give your side of the issue until you have shown the other party you understand their point.

If you are aroused to the point where you can't listen effectively, ask for a break and some time to assimilate what is being said. Either take a break or ask to be the speaker. The other party will then have to be a good listener for you. If you have been a good listener and have understood, you might have a better chance of being heard when you are the speaker.

- **Ask questions.** Paraphrase or summarize the point being said in the most caring way you can. Draw your critic out. Ask for examples. Clarify the problem.

- **Take criticism into account.** Immediate retorts and canned answers that don't take into account what has just been said may cause your critic to redouble their efforts to get through to you. Answers that are not responsive are a signal to the critic to try to make their point again.

- **Don't quibble or get sidetracked.** Even if the points being made are harsh, unfair, exaggerated, or even extreme, ignore the offensive part and try to find the underlying concern. The way it is being said isn't the problem. The problem is the problem. In paraphrasing, deliberately use milder and more benign language to help stay on track.

- **Find a way to agree with what is being said, at least a part of it.** Don't argue against feelings. People are entitled to their feelings whether you agree with them or not. If you disagree, listen carefully to what is being said. Work on forming a bridge from something you agree with them to the areas of disagreement.

If you feel you need to clarify your motives, simply repeat your view without getting angry or defensive.

Part VIII: Negotiation and Problem-Solving

*Communication is not a matter of being right but starting
a flow of energy between two people that can
result in mutual understanding.*
- John A. Sanford.

IS ANGER HAZARDOUS TO RELATIONSHIPS?
CHAPTER FORTY-ONE

Anger is a normal emotion. We experience it when we sense unfairness or injustice. Sometimes we experience it when we feel frustrated, deprived, or when we pass judgment on a situation as being worthy of an angry reaction. Sadly, some of us use anger as a tool to manipulate or intimidate another person to get our way or control the discussion.

Anger generally creates anger in the other party. What starts out as a legitimate attempt to communicate or resolve a difficult problem becomes worse. Anger often prevents clear thinking and interferes with goodwill.

Intimate partners must learn how to manage their anger and control the exchange of negative behavior. Partners in a healthy relationship realize how hurtful their angry barbs can be. They stop short of retaliating with a hurtful comment and find ways of expressing their feelings constructively. They find respectful ways of expressing criticisms and annoyances without resorting to words that hurt - words sometimes not meant - and sadly, words that are remembered.

So what is the purpose of anger? Anger is like pain. It is a warning. Pain tells us that something is wrong in our body and that we need to attend to it in order to take corrective action. People who ignore chronic pain without understanding its source take a chance that the cause of the pain will become aggravated by neglect.

Anger is a good barometer of the emotional system. It alerts us that something is wrong and the cause needs to be pinpointed. Examining our anger helps us look at how our assumptions have been violated or even what our assumptions are. Anger is useful in terms of identifying situations that need to be changed.

Once we understand how we feel and why, then we can choose what to do about it. Anger is the body's way of rebelling against the status quo. It tells us to think. Once we think through the cause, then the solutions are more apparent.

However, attempting to engage in corrective action while angry makes things worse. Actions aren't as well thought out. There is also the strong likelihood that anger will create anger in the other party. This is not a recipe for working out differences.

Venting anger is not productive. Expressing anger creates more anger in the person expressing anger. The theory that venting anger reduces aggression is wrong. According to research by psychologists Brad Bushman and Angela Stack at Iowa State University and Roy Baumeister at Florida State University, venting anger actually increases anger and aggression in subsequent situations.

If people believe that expressing anger is helpful, they don't restrain themselves. Venting anger does not decrease hostility, but instead increases it. People who engage in anger often find it easier to become angry the next time. Anger is a habit that gets worse with use.

Marriage research shows that negative interactions take a toll on marital relationships. The percentage of positive to negative interactions must be overwhelmingly positive for the relationship to absorb the pain, humiliation or unfairness that an angry blow-up is likely to trigger.

Anger violates basic sensitivities about being treated with respect and dignity. The process of communicating suffers when the recipient of the anger reacts to anger instead of the ideas being expressed. Your anger affects the way your partner feels about you. Feeling abused or mistreated in the process discourages attempts to resolve other differences.

Can anger be a good thing? Are there times when a relationship benefits from anger being expressed? Yes. It generally means the motives and intent of the angry person are good. An angry person wants change. Desperately so. It means he or she is trying to break through, even by primitive means, to correct something that he or she feels is wrong.

Anger plays an important role in self-diagnosing and early short-circuiting of hostile conflict. By being aware of one's own emotions, people then can choose to disengage from an argument before anger takes a destructive toll on the relationship. The angry party then can reflect on the cause of his or her anger. When the parties subsequently re-engage their discussion, the angry person then can be more articulate and defined in expressing a complaint.

Expressing anger is good when the other party has enough emotional control to be able to listen to anger. Good listening defuses and de-escalates an angry person. It helps an angry person verbalize and express their frustrations or issues. It helps the angry person feel he or she is being taken seriously or even cared about. It takes a lot of emotional self-discipline not to react to an angry provocation. Only by trying to understand anger is the bridge to communication built. If the listener's arousal level becomes too high or if defensiveness is triggered, then the productive course of action is a time out.

An angry complaint may be unwarranted, misguided, or even meant to hurt. But the mere fact that your spouse said it or believes it makes it important to understand thoroughly. If there is validity to it, and chances are there is a core of truth to his or her perception, your partner is offering you an opportunity to discuss or correct the problem. One of the blessings of marriage is having a loving critic, someone who knows you and is willing to share constructive feedback.

In close relationships, anger can be a prelude to intimacy. Problems are brought out in the open and understood. Solutions are proposed and commitments are made. Reconciliation takes place. Each partner has confidence that the real issues, even those fueled by anger, can be worked out. They draw closer and redefine their relationship.

Anger can be a good thing if used sparingly and expressed under the right circumstances. It is a hazardous, volatile, highly combustible emotion to be used with utmost care by someone who knows how to handle it.

Timeouts and the 24 Hour Rule
Minimize Marital Conflict
Chapter Forty-Two

Incomplete discussions short-circuited by angry outbursts and poor emotional control have a devastating effect on marriage. Too many things are said and done in the middle of heated arguments that are hurtful.

Unless their partner is able to listen to anger, it doesn't do any good for an angry person to vent. Anger generally creates anger. Angry people aren't screening the way they say things. Unfortunate things are said and remembered.

Equally devastating is the icy, cold withdrawal where grudges and resentments are nursed. Days go by. Obvious but veiled anger creates an emotional chasm between a couple. The process of reconciling is awkward and uneven. One partner may habitually be the one to give in and attempt to restore the relationship but without resolution of the disagreement that started the conflict in the first place.

Calling a time out. Couples can minimize conflict by monitoring their anger, body signals, and arousal level. They can ask for a time out until they have emotional control. They may be afraid of their inability to control their anger if the situation escalates in intensity.

In high conflict discussions, it is not just the upset or angry person who has a right to call time out. The person on the receiving end can call time out as well. For the listener, the discussion may become too upsetting. When the listener becomes emotionally overloaded, he or she can no longer listen accurately or empathetically. It is fair to let the speaker know that you are no longer capable of being a good listener.

If two people are upset and angry at the same time, nobody is listening. The point of communication is to hear and understand each other. An angry person wants to be heard, not argued with or even reasoned with. Both parties need to be able to call time out on a problematic discussion and have that time out request respected without debate about whether it is fair or necessary.

Marital conflicts often take the form of a "pursuer," who is anxious and wants to resolve conflict immediately, and a "withdrawer," who may not be good at thinking on his or her feet and needs time to assimilate information, regulate emotions, or collect thoughts. Neither style is inherently wrong; they just happen to not match up well. They frustrate each other.

"Time outs" as control. There is also a control issue. The person who controls what is and isn't talked about has power in the relationship. Sometimes a spouse will call time out, not as a good faith effort to gain emotional control, but as a ploy to derail a discussion he or she doesn't want to have. The issue isn't worked through and the status quo is maintained. Some marriage partners are suspicious that a request for a time out is an unfair way of avoiding a discussion that might result in change.

The 24 hour rule. In order for a time out to be an effective tool there must be an equally binding and respected rule that the couple bring up the dispute within 24 hours of the time out request. This is middle ground between the pursuer and withdrawer. The scales aren't weighted unfairly to favor one style over the other.

Some couples have a rule that they never go to bed angry. While laudable, this may not be feasible in terms of when arguments start. It may not give enough time for the angry person to gain control. It is a good idea to not start a conflict discussion after 9:00 p.m. There must be enough time to work out a problem without interfering with sleep.

Resuming the discussion. Twenty-four hours is usually sufficient time to calm down and be approachable on the same topic. The 24 hour rule is a maximum time frame, not a minimum. It might take only 15 minutes for the angry or upset person to calm down and resume the discussion.

The discretion on when to resume the discussion should be left to the person who called it. If possible, the parties could decide right then when the best time would be to resume their discussion. Setting a time is courteous, but not always possible, depending on the emotional level of the upset person.

A person who is angry or frustrated needs to use time out effectively and analyze the root causes of his or her anger. This reflection time will help the spouse articulate his or her concerns in a clear manner without anger or strong emotion interfering with the communication process. A time out also gives time for reflection on the other party's point of view so that a balanced discussion can take place.

Both rules are necessary. When a 24 hour rule is a trusted part of a couple's conflict resolution repertoire, the anxious partner who is feeling disadvantaged by incomplete discussions can relax and feel confident that important topics will be talked through eventually. This rule is just as important for the partner who is cut off as the rule is for the partner who is flooded with emotion. Both rules need to be honored for angry partners to resolve their conflicts.

WHEN A MAN WON'T TALK
CHAPTER FORTY-THREE

A common complaint by women about men in marriage is that they withdraw during arguments and refuse to discuss issues that are important. When this becomes a pattern in marriage, it is destructive and often intensifies conflict between them. The wife pursues and the man runs away.

Women, if asked about their anger, explain that they are not angry but are trying to discuss, in an animated way, an issue of vital importance to themselves and the relationship. They feel they are trying to resolve a difference between them - and that their mate over-interprets their emotion as anger.

If women do acknowledge their anger, they explain that it is an attempt to break through when all other methods of communicating have failed. Their anger demonstrates their care and anxiety to make a change in their relationship. It also indicates their level of frustration with the inability to engage in a problem-solving process with their spouse. They come to feel that their husbands' failure to respond to their concerns is a calculated way of maintaining power or control in the marriage.

Why men run away. It is true that some men use withdrawal to control the agenda of what gets talked about and what doesn't. However, for some men, there is another explanation. Men may be wired to fight the sabre-toothed tiger but they feel helpless in the face of a female "assault" where force is not an option. They don't know how to deal with a woman's anger, tears or biting criticism. Instead of reacting back with anger, calmly listening to their spouse, or engaging in a dialogue about the issue at hand, they retreat.

A man on the receiving end of these angry complaints feels hurt, angry or defensive. His wife is well-armed with a litany of well thought out complaints, weaknesses and failures described in vivid and graphic detail. Her memory for past hurts is unforgivingly precise.

His explanations in the past haven't been good enough. When he has tried to explain himself he has dug an even deeper hole. He feels out-argued and out-matched by his righteously indignant and verbally skilled wife.

So what does he do? He does like other brave, masculine compatriots of his gender would do - he withdraws. He sulks. He gets even by not cooperating.

Even if he feels his wife's pain, he can't bring himself to comfort her because of his own wounded pride and martyred self-pity. Being macho, he doesn't let on how badly he is hurt by her cutting remarks or his sense of helplessness to communicate his side of the matter. He just hopes the issue will go away. He slips into a sanctuary of silence.

Why women pursue. How does a woman react to a man who dismisses her and refuses to have a dialogue about her concerns? She becomes more angry and frustrated. His unwillingness to talk to her about her concerns makes her wonder if he doesn't care. She feels lonely and neglected.

So what does she do? She steps up the pressure. She tries to break through with greater force and insistence. Her efforts to communicate her unhappiness and displeasure result in more withdrawal and camouflaged combat that spread to other aspects of their marriage.

Breaking the pattern. If you are a woman in this type of scenario, what would you do to break this escalating pattern of anger, withdrawal and poor problem-solving? Getting angry and confrontational doesn't work.

1. Talk less and listen more. Listen to his feelings and draw him out in an atmosphere that is safe. Summarize his concerns in a caring way and show him you understand the point he is trying to make. Let him know that you respect his opinion and that it matters what he thinks.

Don't come across as always being "right." Be open to influence by what he says. Consider his ideas before responding. Don't interrupt. Let him explain himself fully before asking for the floor. Put yourself in his shoes and show empathy for the position he perceives himself to be in.

2. Ask open-ended questions. "So what do you think?" or, "Why do you think that happened?" Be curious. Spend time getting to know his logic. Don't react with disbelief or negative body language. Take your time and get to the bottom of his thinking before giving a counter-argument or position.

3. Stay calm. Practice a slow, soft warm-up to the issue at hand. Express your positive intent to resolve difficulties and reaffirm your love before launching off into your side of the issue. Voice your complaints and concerns with a calm tone of voice. Remember, it is your anger that intimidates him.

4. Express your appreciation. After a discussion, express appreciation for discussing the matter with you. Reaffirm your love again.

What is the husband's responsibility? He needs to verbalize his side of the issue. He has to do his part to open up the dialogue. He has to trust that his wife will be open-minded and treat his point-of-view with respect.

He has to learn to listen to anger or emotion without overreacting. Listening means summarizing her points in a caring way. Being willing to work with her on problems gives her hope that changes she needs in the relationship can be negotiated - and so can his. His caring and concern shown through listening when she is upset comes across as love.

DON'T ARGUE - NEGOTIATE!
CHAPTER FORTY-FOUR

Do you know my friends, Ted and Alice? They argue all the time. Money. Parenting. Sex. Relatives. Religion. Basic roles and responsibilities. Autonomy. Destructive habits. Worst of all, they don't get anywhere. It's like they're spinning their wheels on a patch of ice. If they could only hit solid ground, maybe they could get somewhere. It all comes from their strongly held beliefs and values about what is the right way to live. Compromise is impossible.

Persistent disagreements and conflict may be a sign of poor communication and problem-solving skills. Marital partners may have their blind spots and may not know how to make their arguments productive. The more different they are, the better their communication skills need to be.

There are loving, trusting, respectful ways of solving problems together. Ted and Alice, in their anxiety to achieve goals, use anger and resentment as tools to get their way. They don't know enough about how to resolve conflict as they strive toward working out their differences.

Conflict is normal. It is a fact of life. We are different. We have different backgrounds. We learn basic values and views about life in our childhood family. In early marriage there is competition to see whose values will continue in the new family. One of the challenges of marriage is to accept differences in personality, background and motivation and then to work out common purposes, dreams and ways of doing things.

Our motives may be different, and most likely, so are our methods. In close relationships, and in business or professional life, our goals vary from one another. One can scarcely imagine a day without some form of conflict.

Conflict is neither positive nor negative. Resolution can move in either direction. It is how we handle conflict that makes it an opportunity instead of being a hurtful or divisive experience. We need a way to address our fear of conflict. Our lives are improved when we understand conflict and have tools to resolve it.

Why can conflict be a good thing? Conflict indicates genuine concern. It represents the values underlying emotions and strong positions. Emotions, even anger, are a sign that the people involved care.

Conflict shows engagement. People feel safe enough to bring up their ideas with the goal of working through their differences. For this to occur, the process has to be respectful and courteous. Conflict gives us a chance to clarify our own emotions and values - and those with whom we are in conflict.

Although conflict avoidance can be a good strategy on occasion, if a problem isn't confronted, conflict can escalate and easily grow in intensity and magnitude.

When conflict helps participants address concerns that are larger in scope than the narrow interests of a select few, better ideas and solutions are generated.

Conflict tests a couple's ability to communicate and solve problems, especially when emotions run high. Long-running arguments and conflict may be a sign of poor communication and problem-solving skills. This is what couples like Ted and Alice need to learn about negotiations and conflict resolution.

Try exploring interests. In their book, *Getting to Yes,* Roger Fisher and William Ury emphasize the importance of "exploring interests" as opposed to "defending a position." Exploring interests means finding out the perceptions, motivations and desires of the other party. It is the art of asking good questions and really listening to the answers.

Recognize that your partner's concerns are valid and show you are interested in reaching a solution that meets both your needs. You need to identify and explain your position so your partner can understand your point of view.

Ted and Alice often jump too quickly into finding solutions without taking time to really understand each other. They could resolve many of their problems through understanding alone.

Whose standards should be used? Fisher and Ury suggest using information found outside the family as guidelines for fair and valid agreements. What is commonly done and considered fair by others? What do the experts say?

Searching for acceptable standards independently of the will and desires of each other can be used to evaluate agreements or which options to consider. Just as Ted should try to be open-minded toward Alice's interests, he should also be open-minded to the standards she feels are fair.

Try inventing options. The question becomes, "Now that we agree on what is wrong, what can we do about it?" It is time to brainstorm alternatives. This is the creative part of problem-solving.

The purpose of inventing several options is to reconcile interests. Behind every opposing position, couples have many more shared interests than conflicting ones. The challenge is to build on these common positions.

Separating the process of inventing options from deciding options is important. Decision-making and commitments come later. This is an open-ended time when each partner should feel the freedom to brainstorm and make suggestions. Don't narrow the gap - broaden the options.

Ted and Alice need to spend time thinking through the solution to each other's problem. An solution that comes at the expense of just one partner will not be effective. An attitude of being willing to satisfy each others' interests will lead to long-term answers. Specify alternatives that are acceptable. Be open and receptive to each other's ideas. Acknowledge a positive behavior or thought. Reinforce any movement toward an agreement. Alleviate fears. **Don't be too quick to solve problems.** Solutions come after understanding. The rule of thumb is to spend at least half the time exploring interests and inventing options before starting the task of coming to an agreement.

Respect each other's need to think about what was said. Time is needed to deal with any emotions felt or expressed during the process of exploring interests. Discussions often fall apart when couples rush to find a solution before they understand what their partners' issues really are. Get to an agreement on what the problem is and *then* brainstorm for alternatives, options, and solutions.

Come to an agreement. Try hypothetical statements as trial balloons. There are many ways of resolving conflict - compromise, accommodation, declaring a moratorium, agreeing to disagree, and collaboration. Each can be successful.

Pros and cons are weighed. A decision needs to be made and commitments given toward a specific plan.

Agreements should be tentative until the framework of the agreement is in place. Nothing important should be left out. Any areas where disagreements still exist should be identified. Couples shouldn't get bogged down on details before agreement on the main issues. Use of hypothetical or contingent offers narrows the gap to closure.

Ted and Alice must fill in the details and fine tune the agreement before making a final commitment. A lasting agreement should be practical, easily understood and easy to follow through. It should have objective standards for judging if it is working. In the end, finding a way to be generous will end negotiations on a good note.

Both partners reach a point of being able to give their commitment to this question, "Yes, this is our agreement."

Set a time to review and evaluate the agreement. Ted and Alice start their plan on a trial basis. They set aside time to review how it is working and to make any necessary adjustments. If they follow through and honor their commitments, this sets the stage for further problem-solving in a relationship of trust.

The benefits. This is the beauty of problem-solving as a couple. As you develop a track record of being successful at bringing up hard problems and solving them, you will be willing to trust the process. You will be able to fine tune your relationship to greater compatibility. You will be closer and more intimate.

If you master these negotiating skills, your differences will still be challenging, but not necessarily threatening. From time to time, you'll surprise each other on how really different you are...and always will be. Then again, it might be even more surprising how alike you've become. Most of all you will learn to trust that thorny problems can be solved through a loving and respectful search for middle ground.

Continuing a working relationship. Roger Fisher and Scott Brown in their book, *Getting Together*, feel that a primary goal of negotiation in an ongoing relationship is to finish the negotiations so that each party feels good about the process. How your partner feels about you after you have discussed an issue is more important than the particular outcome.

HE SAYS, SHE SAYS: BUT DO THEY UNDERSTAND?

CHAPTER FORTY-FIVE

What do women want? Men can't figure that out. What do men want? Women understand but would like some changes. One main source of confusion is in the different styles men and women use in conversation. Men and women differ in language and willingness to share emotions.

Communications: Men and women speak differently. In her book, *You Just Don't Understand,* Debra Tannen advanced a two-culture theory of miscommunications. The basic premise was that men engage in "report" talk - "to preserve independence and negotiate and maintain status in a hierarchical social order." Women use "rapport" talk as "a way of establishing connection and negotiating relationships."

A similar book, by linguist Robin Lakoff, *Talking Power: The Language of Politics,* explores the two-culture idea from the idea of power. He sees language differences not as a gender issue but as a power issue. West concludes, *"Men's language is the language of the powerful. It is meant to be direct, clear, succinct, and would be expected of those who need not fear giving offense . . . It is the language of people who are in charge of making observable changes in the real world.*

"Women's language developed as a way of surviving and even flourishing without control over economic, physical or social reality. Then it is necessary to listen more than speak, agree more than confront, be delicate, be indirect, say dangerous things in such a way their impact will be felt after the speaker is out of range of the hearer's retaliation."

Woman's language evolved to persuade and influence rather than to assert and demand. Women are skilled at anticipating what others want or need. It is a language to placate the powerful and soothe ruffled feathers. This language is oriented toward cooperation and attention to the news, gossip and feelings of others.

Women speak more tentatively with men than they do with other women. They offer more disclaimers, more modesty, more hedged statements, more moderating terms, more tag questions and more hesitations. They attend to feelings and are more polite in their unwillingness to interrupt the speaker.

Why? Psychologist Linda Carli, Wellesley College found that women are more influential with men when they use indirect and tentative communications, than if they speak directly. When women do this, men like them more and find them more trustworthy. Men are more inclined to listen if they sense women are not challenging their status.

Women can speak the male dialect. They certainly do so in business and professional settings. Males are less able to switch to female speech.

My own experience in counseling couples is that men especially need to learn the intimate language of relationships rather than use the language of the workplace. These are precisely the skills that women have honed in their lives. By learning to speak tentatively, the speaker communicates more respect, consideration and equality than by the direct style that men typically use.

Why don't men talk more? As boys and adolescents, men learn a side-by-side style of intimacy. Men use physical gestures, laugh at each other's jokes and do one another favors. There is a lot of teasing, in-group jokes, humor and horsing around. It is a male way of disguising affection and closeness. Men associate intimacy with being together and being relaxed and comfortable around one another. Men equate intimacy and love with action -- doing things for others. Intimacy is defined as being helpful, doing useful work, being a protector and a provider, and putting the wishes of the family ahead of their own.

The image of masculinity is to be strong, silent, assertive and competent. Men are expected to have self-control -- to remain calm and stoic under pressure. They learn to inhibit emotions so they can engage in problem solving. They hide their weaknesses, fears, anxiety, sadness and grief.

Men have a difficult time with conflict while women have a harder time with emotional distance. Generally, men withdraw from high conflict situations while women are more likely to want an immediate resolution through discussion.

What do women want? Talk. Deep talk. Small talk. They want men to reveal their feelings and to be vulnerable -- not an easy task for a man. Women were raised with face-to-face, heart-to-heart exchanges with their girlfriends. Women are almost eager to reveal weaknesses, foibles and fears without hesitancy. No male ego here.

By sharing feelings, women experience relief from stress, feel better and gain ideas for self-improvement. It is a way of bonding. A "girls night out" has utter frankness and personal self-disclosure that would make most men cringe -- and probably blush.

A female view of intimacy places greater emphasis on talking and expressing one's affection and admiration. For men, the purpose of talking about feelings and problems is to solve them.

When women bring up a feeling or problem with their male partner, they expect confirmation, understanding and listening. What do they get? Advice! Her spouse immediately assumes her sharing of feelings is a request for help. He stops listening and starts to be helpful. Wrong! What his wife wants is confirmation, understanding and a sounding board for her thoughts.

What is needed is the ability to do both languages. Men can learn the language of intimacy. Women can be sensitive and more accepting of male stoicism and playfulness. By understanding each other's worlds, we can accept each other's gifts and give more of what the other wants.

BUILDING TRUST BY HONORING AGREEMENTS
CHAPTER FORTY-SIX

How do we build trust? Better yet, how do we rebuild trust as we fall short of complete reliability in our word and deed? Jack Rosenblum, EdD, JD, of Deerfield, Massachusetts shares ideas on the way we enter and keep agreements as being a key factor in the development of trust in close relationships.

Rosenblum believes that trust hinges on four main principles: *openness, honesty, respect* and *credibility,* all of which are under-girded by consistency.

- **Openness.** Openness is sharing things about oneself so that others know what you are thinking and feeling. If they don't know, they will guess and perhaps guess wrong. If they err, they might err on the self-protective side. A closed or secretive person leaves a lot to the imagination. Trust is harder to form.

- **Honesty.** Trust starts and ends with honesty. Lies and dishonesty destroy trust. Honest feedback, for better or worse, is important in helping others understand the impact of their behavior on others. A true friend has the courage to tell the truth with compassion.

- **Respect.** Respect means hearing and understanding others, acknowledging the greatness in them, recognizing their positive intentions, and disagreeing without making them feel "wrong." We value their rights and opinions as equals. We seek to understand and resolve problems to our mutual satisfaction. In giving respect, we earn respect.

- **Credibility**. Credibility means that we are taken at our word. We build our credibility by reliably doing the things we say we are going to do. Every time we fail to do something we said we would do, we chip away at our credibility. It is that simple.

Rosenblum elaborates on how couples can enhance or destroy their trust by how they handle agreements. He gives four rules governing the making and keeping of agreements that had a profound life-changing affect in his own life.

1. Make only those agreements that you intend to keep. Most of us are guilty of over-promising what we intend to do. Sometimes we make a casual commitment not really expecting to follow through. Be extremely careful about which agreements you make and follow through on the ones you do make.

Trust is established by the seriousness by which you take the request and the straight-forward manner of dealing with it. Your spouse loses trust by responding to requests in a vague or untimely way.

2. Don't make or accept fuzzy agreements. Rosenblum found that his own frustration with others and himself was really his problem because of the lack of clarity in his agreements. By specifying the expectations precisely, he found that confusion around fuzzy agreements was cleared up.

When his wife told him she would meet him "around" 3:00 p.m., she meant anytime between 3:00 p.m. and 3:30 p.m. His idea of "around" 3:00 p.m. meant 3:00 p.m. sharp. By adding clarity to their agreement, they avoided frustration and conflict.

3. Give the earliest possible notice when an agreement needs to be broken or renegotiated. Life isn't always predictable. Things come up. Stuff happens. Agreements need to be renegotiated. You owe it to the other party to let them know as soon as possible if you have a change of circumstances. It is a common courtesy. Early notice doesn't hurt your credibility. Late notice does.

4. Clean up broken agreements. Take the initiative in acknowledging a broken agreement. Don't let it fade into the woodwork. Your spouse notices. It hurts your credibility. Do this as soon as it is feasible. Explain the circumstances and apologize if necessary. "What do I have to do to get back in your good graces?"

If someone has broken an agreement with you, approach him or her and initiate a discussion. Clear up the matter as best as you can. If this person indicates he can be counted on in future agreements, forgive him and restore the relationship.

It makes a difference. How would your relationship with your partner be different if you practiced these four principles of making agreements all the time? Some of the benefits might include the elimination of confusion, clearing up old resentments and avoiding new ones, less guilt, less over-commitment, more responsibility to each other and more clarity about boundaries and obligations.

An agreement on how to handle agreements would be a benefit to most marriages. Another difficulty in arriving at agreements is when requests are not answered or when there is a lack of clarity or timeliness in giving an answer. More care needs to be taken before agreements are made.

A request is a straight forward attempt to solicit an agreement or an answer. Many times, problems in relationships develop when one partner knowingly or unwittingly refuses to answer, changes the topic or gives a vague, "I'll think about it."

No answer takes a toll on the relationship. Rosenblum suggests four ways of responding to a request that maintain respect and avoid misunderstandings.

1. "Yes, I will and here's when." Be careful when you give this answer. Your credibility is on the line. Only make agreements that you intend to keep.

Some people say yes when they mean no. Sometimes the assent is a casual gesture by someone being "nice" and isn't meant to be a real commitment. There is a big difference between, "You can count on it," and lip service meant to assuage or put off the listener.

Some people say yes without giving it enough thought. A yes could mean, "Maybe," or, "I'll think about it." The person making the request doesn't understand that the "yes" is meant as a way of buying time.

The "here's when" makes the agreement crystal clear. Without a time frame, the "yes" will seem fuzzy. If there is confusion about when a promise will be fulfilled, assumptions can be made that it is already a broken promise.

Some of us are guilty of over-promising what we intend to do. Be extremely careful about which agreements you make and follow through on the ones you do make.

2. "No, I won't and here is why." This is a bona-fide answer. It is difficult to turn down a request. Generally we want to please others. But circumstances might preclude our ability to do what is requested. It is fair to the person making the request to let him or her know that. Also, we may choose not to fill the request because of previous commitments, out of principle, or because it doesn't fit our priorities.

The "here's why" is part of a respectful answer. Most of the time, people are entitled to an explanation. An opportunity is given for the petitioner to be persuasive and try to change the answer as the objections are raised. These attempts should be limited.

After a "no" is given and the petitioner keeps on trying to make his or her case, the recipient can summarize the persuasive argument to show he or she understands it and that repeated attempts to make the same case are unnecessary. He or she can also give the "I need time to think about it" as a way of thoughtfully considering the request, even though the likely answer will still be no.

Persistent attempts to change a "no" into a "yes" come across as nagging. A "no" is an answer, a respectful answer, and needs to be accepted -- not treated as the beginning of an argument.

3. "I will under these conditions." This answer paves the way for a "yes" that is realistic and takes into account all of the objections, mitigating challenges or circumstances. A conditional "maybe" makes for better agreements than an easy "yes" that may not be honored.

When the recipient spells out the problems or the challenges to be overcome, the petitioner hears them and can counter-propose actions that might overcome the difficulties. This sets the stage for negotiations and cooperation in solving problems. The recipient hears ideas on how the problems might be overcome and thoughtfully considers the petitioner's thoughts.

It is a fair answer. It is one that leads to realistic plans or to a clearer discussion of why "no" might be the best answer.

4. "I need to think about it and I will get back to you at such and such a time." Some people don't think well on their feet. Emotions might be involved. Others need to review their schedules or gather further information before they can give a yes or a no.

Some answers take time to consider, so if the answer is yes, it is realistic. A no that is thoughtfully given after full and careful consideration is respectful. Without a time frame for the eventual answer, the person making the request eventually figures out that he or she didn't get an answer and ask again. This is not nagging. It is asking for an answer.

Giving a specific time also makes, "I need time to think about it," a legitimate answer. To leave it vague without a time frame is not a complete answer to the request. Too many people use "I need time to think about it" as a polite or face-saving way of saying "no."

In some situations that is probably OK, but in a close relationship, a time frame helps both parties know that the eventual answer will be a good one. Perhaps the answer will be a conditional yes and move to a more thorough discussion of how or under what circumstances an agreement will work.

WHAT THE BATTLE OF THE SEXES IS ALL ABOUT
CHAPTER FORTY-SEVEN

One of the ongoing struggles between couples is finding a satisfying level of closeness (intimacy) or distance (autonomy) that each partner wants in a relationship. When one partner's need for intimacy is not realized, he or she presses for change through emotional demands, criticism and complaints. The other partner retreats through withdrawal, defensiveness and passive inaction.

This pattern of interaction has been variously labeled the "demand/withdraw," "pursuer/distancer" or the "intrusion/rejection" pattern by the researchers who have studied it.

Andrew Christensen and his colleagues at UCLA have found that partners who want more closeness tend to be the demanders while partners who want more autonomy tend to be the withdrawers. Women tend to be demanders while men tend to be withdrawers.

Why are women usually in the demand role while men tend to withdraw as a way of handling conflict? Christiansen offers these explanations:

The socialization explanation. Women are trained to be social and expressive and more likely to fear abandonment and rejection. A woman's identity is developed in a context of relationships. She is more likely to be threatened by separation.

Men are trained to be independent and strong and are more likely to fear intrusion and engulfment. A man's identity is developed in a context of separation. He is more likely to be threatened by intimacy and attachment.

The biological explanation. Men are physiologically more reactive to stress than women. They can't handle conflict as well because of their higher levels of emotional arousal. They try to avoid conflict, withdraw from conflict or reconcile conflict quickly.

Women are less reactive to stress than men, especially in interpersonal conflict when the atmosphere between them becomes hostile or confrontational. Women are more likely than men to escalate conflict. They are more comfortable expressing their hurt and anger. Women are conflict-confronting while men are conflict-avoiding.

The difference in power explanation. Men historically enjoy greater benefits in traditional marriage. Women carry the burden of household and child care responsibilities, even when both spouses are employed full time.

Men are likely to be a conservative force in relationships, with a vested interest in preserving the status quo. Men are more able to structure a relationship to their desires than are women. Women are more dissatisfied with the status quo and pressure for change, while men attempt to keep the status quo by withdrawing and avoiding confrontation.

Is the demand role a function of lack of power in a relationship? Or do differences in biology/socialization predispose women to take a demanding role in order to meet their needs for intimacy?

Christensen and his associates devised a study to answer this question.

Thirty-one couples were assessed in two conflict situations: one in which the husband wanted change in his wife and the second in which the wife wanted change in her husband.

They found that "wife-demand/husband withdraw" interaction was more likely than a "husband-demand/wife-withdraw" pattern. In general, men were disposed to withdraw during conflict. When placed in a role of wanting change, men and women were equally demanding. However, when a husband raised an issue for his wife to change, she was more willing to be open to her husband's complaints than he was when it was her issue.

Christensen explains that in the conflict between a desire for more intimacy and a desire for autonomy, the person wanting to avoid intimacy has a distinct power advantage. *"Autonomy can be achieved unilaterally; closeness requires joint desire and cooperation...The compromise between the two will favor the person who wants less closeness."*

The change may not be good enough for one partner, and the pressure for change continues. The other partner feels his or her autonomy threatened and increases resistance. The person who wants less has more power to control the relationship.

Christensen continues, *"If women want more from relationships than men and are more dependent on relationship satisfaction than men, women as a result may be at a power disadvantage relative to men."* A man who wishes to avoid intimacy is inherently empowered when pitted against a woman who wants more intimacy.

When a man wants change in a relationship, a woman is usually willing to listen, negotiate and work on their differences. On the other hand, when a woman wants change, a man is much more likely to ignore the problem. A wife resorts to complaints and demands. He withdraws. She persists. And the battle goes on.

How can the "demand/withdraw" pattern be changed to a pattern of cooperation, mutuality, empathy, dialogue and problem-solving?

Problem. One partner avoids conflict and consequently, problem solving, because of his or her own emotional arousal when the partner shows anger and other negative emotions.

Research has shown that men are more likely to take conflict-avoiding positions in disagreements while women feel more comfort in expressing emotion in an emotionally-charged atmosphere.

Solution. The person wanting change needs to bring up and discuss problems in calm, unemotional, non-threatening ways. Respectful, mannerly communication softens the impact and minimizes defensiveness. This shows respect for the "withdrawer's" emotional limits.

On the other hand, it may be just as hard for the "demander" to contain and channel his or her feelings. The withdrawer can take active steps to ease the distress of the demander by being willing to listen and understand the problem.

Problem. The lack of problem-solving because of the "demand/withdraw" pattern takes its toll on one of the partners. The dissatisfied partner steps up the pressure only to encounter more resistance.

Solution. The couple can benefit by a communication exercise where one partner takes a "speaker" role and the other partner a "listener" role. After a period of time, roles are reversed. The "avoidant" partner takes a turn in the speaker role - whether it is wanted or not - and shares feelings and opinions in an atmosphere where he or she gains a fair hearing.

The possibility of a genuine dialogue is created by the mutual exchange of feelings. The clear speaker/listener guidelines equalize power between the couple. The underlying conflict is addressed and the demand lessens.

Sometimes couples need assistance from a third party to improve their communication and problem-solving skills. It takes skill to be able to listen to emotionally arousing material and refrain from inserting one's point of view.

Problem. The person with less investment and/or more resources uses power tactics to get his or her needs met while not expending much effort to meet the needs of the partner. The emotionally dependent partner tries a variety of strategies to correct the imbalance in the relationship.

Solution. The demand/withdraw cycle can be broken when the "avoidant" partner aggressively meets the needs of the mate and trusts that his or her own needs will be met without reliance on the inherent power advantage in the relationship.

When a spouse consistently shows anxious concern for the well being of one's partner and lovingly meets those needs, demands will fade or will be expressed more lovingly. When needs are being met, power differences in the couple are minimized and cooperation, negotiation and mutual decision-making follow.

For trust to develop, each partner surrenders the ability to secure his or her interests. A spouse chooses to become vulnerable to the goodwill and benevolence of his or her mate. Trust is the opposite of control.

If there is trust that one's needs will be taken into account, then a partner's behavior will be judged as well-intended. It will be seen as truly caring rather than as a power move to gain one's self-interest. In high trust relationships, an attempt to influence is seen as an effort to solve a problem. In low trust relationships, the same behavior is seen as an attempt to control.

Problem: One partner in a conflict situation may be anxious, angry, aroused or insecure and wants the conflict to be resolved immediately. On the other hand, the partner feels overwhelmed, needs time to think and process the conflict or may be avoiding conflict. He or she feels unprepared or at a disadvantaged trying to resolve conflict under high emotional conditions. Each partner frustrates the other by trying to impose his or her style of conflict resolution (demand/withdraw) on the other.

Solution: Either party has the option of requesting an immediate disengagement of the argument and the other has to immediately and graciously cooperate. By doing so they are also agreeing to re-engage in the same discussion within a 24 hour time frame. This buys time for the withdrawer to think and time for the demander to moderate his or her emotions and to know that the issue will get a reasonably quick hearing. This is middle ground between two conflicting styles.

If you don't get the changes you want on your own, you may want to try a professional marriage counselor to break the demand-withdraw pattern.

Part IX: Love On The Rocks

*The change women want most is for men to talk
about their feelings, and the change men want most is to
be understood without having to talk about their feelings.*
- Michael McGill

TEN SURE-FIRE WAYS TO LOUSE UP
A GOOD MARRIAGE
CHAPTER FORTY-EIGHT

What's that you say - not enough trouble in your life? Are you looking for big time marital problems? You've come to the right place. Here are ten tried and true ways -- tested by many couples -- for creating exquisite pain and unhappiness.

1. Be selfish. Put your own wants, needs, ideas, work and agenda consistently ahead of your spouse's. Expect love but don't give it. Toss out a few crumbs once in a while when the pressure is on but quickly revert back to being Master or Mistress of the Universe.

Make all major decisions alone. Stall. Flat out refuse to cooperate. Refuse even to discuss it. Keep everything on your terms.

You can get away with being a jerk for years, and by the time your spouse finally decides to pull the plug, he or she will have concluded that you aren't capable of being anything else. At this point all your kind, loving, sensitive acts will be taken as pure manipulation. Don't expect him or her to believe your desperate attempts to change.

2. Be stubborn. Right is right, by darn. You don't have to compromise - never. Protect your ego at all costs. Don't back down.

It's hard being perfect in an imperfect world. Shift the blame if you need to. When in doubt, attack.

Don't respond to criticism. Refuse to change. So what if you have an uncontrolled problem with alcohol, swearing, temper, spending or some other self-destructive and obnoxious behavior. There is no truth you can learn about yourself, least of all from someone who is supposed to take you "as is."

3. Shut her out. (For men only.) Women have a big hang up with communications and feelings. That is their problem. Clam up. Keep your problems to yourself. Being a good provider is enough. You don't have to listen to her. Come home tired. Read the paper. Watch TV. Go to bed early. Avoid anything personal.

4. Don't solve problems. Don't learn how to listen. Interrupt. Bring up the past. Save something juicy for a tough spot. Change the subject. Blow up - easily. Stomp out of the room. Refuse to talk about a problem. Criticize your partner's ideas. Argue without trying to understand your partner's point of view.

5. Bear a grudge. (For women especially.) Never forget an injustice. Cite chapter and verse of every detail of five or six horrid examples of brutish behavior. The past is important. He was, is, and will always be indisputably guilty of extraordinary insensitivity. Imply that nothing has changed. If anything appears remotely connected, trot out your proofs.

6. Act like nothing happened. (Men pay attention.) Never say you're sorry. Act as though anything you did longer than five minutes ago is ancient history and not worthy of comment. You don't have to explain anything. Imply that any mention of anything you may have done in the past is grossly unfair. You don't have to listen to that crap.

7. Take him or her for granted. There is no need to be considerate or appreciative. Withhold your expressions of love. Never say a kind word. Tear down when necessary. Don't respond to requests. Let your relationship dry up out of a lack of attention. Don't go out of your way for your spouse. Settle into a routine. Bridle at the mention of romance. Let time take its toll. Apathy is the opposite of love, not hate.

8. Be angry and abusive. (Partner A) Try to solve your problem immediately, no matter how angry you are. Take it as an insult if your partner tries to cool off or discontinue the argument. Vent your feelings. Don't worry about what you say in anger. If you want to speed up a disaster, get physical.

(Partner B) Walk off at the first sign of trouble. Nurse a grudge. Give the silent treatment. Wear down your partner by refusing to deal with him or her in his or her angry state. Make your partner feel like a jerk for bringing up problems. If you're lucky, you can stay in control of the marriage.

9. Assume your partner's needs for affection are not legitimate. Your way is the right way. Your partner is either a sex maniac or cold cucumber.

(For men) Any touching or caressing can mean only one thing. The bedroom - right away. Don't pay attention to mood, loving behavior or nurturing the relationship. Take any rejection as a personal affront. Keep the pressure on.

(For women) Don't go out of your way to please your partner. He doesn't deserve it. Withhold favors. His tough male ego can handle it - no big deal.

(For both) Persistent problems with premature ejaculation, impotence and incomplete arousal can be solved on one's own. Let time take its course. You'll both get so frustrated, it will be a relief to get away from each other.

10. Don't seek help. Don't go for counseling. Let your pride get in the way. It is better to lose a marriage than face that brand of humiliation. Pointedly refuse to go until your partner is on the absolute verge of divorce and then go. At that time, complain to high heaven and everyone else who will listen that you are not being given a chance.

There you have it folks. Ten surefire ways to raise hackles in your marriage. It is amazing how many folks stumble into these principles without half trying. See you in counseling - if you make it that far.

NOT COMPATIBLE? HERE'S HOW YOU CAN START ENJOYING EACH OTHER AGAIN
CHAPTER FORTY-NINE

Couples grow apart because of individual lifestyle choices, parenting demands and work responsibilities. They don't have that much in common. They stop enjoying each other's company and find it easier to fight when friction occurs between them. What was once a relationship that gave them great pleasure has become a source of pain or disillusionment.

Why we make poor negotiators. Psychologist Bill Harley, Jr., of White Bear Lake, MN, believes that poor marital habits develop when decisions are made during one of three conditions.

1. One condition is when one partner, during a state of emotional intimacy, attempts to please their partner out of self-sacrifice and at their own expense.

2. A second condition occurs when decisions are made during a state of conflict. These decisions are not usually fair and benefit one spouse at the expense of the other. Worse yet, often during conflict, disagreements can be full of demands, disrespect and anger.

3. The third condition is withdrawal. When confronted with a spouse's self-centered and thoughtless behavior, one or both parties decide to withdraw and become emotionally distant. The withdrawn partner protects him or herself from being emotionally vulnerable and stops making efforts to meet his or her partner's emotional needs.

Policy of joint agreement. In all three conditions or states of mind, spouses are not good negotiators and do not produce fair agreements. Couples need a rule that produces fair agreements when their short-sighted instincts encourage them to be unfair. They need a policy of joint agreement. The policy of joint agreement is, "Never do anything without an enthusiastic agreement between you and your spouse."

That means that all decisions have to meet the test of making both you and your spouse happy. Decisions have to be in both your best interests. It gives you and your spouse veto power over decisions that cause unhappiness.

A policy of joint agreement prevents bad habits from getting started. It targets eliminating existing habits and hurts that cause unhappiness. It forces a solution to marital conflicts by encouraging couples to take each other's feelings and perspective into account simultaneously - even when they don't feel like it.

The more compatible a couple is, the easier the negotiating process will be. Harley believes that if a couple follows this policy for a year, they will become compatible and replace their old bad habits with good habits.

Guidelines for successful negotiations. Certain ground rules are necessary for negotiations to be safe and pleasant.

- Smile and be as pleasant and cheerful as possible.
- Avoid selfish demands, disrespectful judgments, angry outbursts, dishonesty, threats, and thoughtless remarks.
- If you reach an impasse or cannot be pleasant or safe, stop negotiating and come back to the issue later.
- Engage in active listening. Understand and respect each other's perspectives before attempting to find a solution.
- Brainstorm with abandon.
- Choose a solution both of you can be enthusiastic about.

Overcoming objections. The policy of joint agreement forces people to make compatible decisions that take both spouses into account. Couples have to dig deeper, be more persuasive, be more flexible and search for new solutions that meet the test.

According to Harley, a couple should spend at least 15 hours a week in "couples" time. This should be the best and most enjoyable time of the week. Couples should choose to do things together that are mutually enjoyable. They can make up lists of activities and negotiate for enthusiastic agreement.

Couples should start by picking smaller, more inconsequential decisions to practice on before moving on to more emotionally-laden conflicts. He recommends going to a grocery store and filling the cart with food items you both agree on. Vetoing an item doesn't mean control or making someone do something they don't want; it means helping each other be thoughtful about how decisions affect each other.

By using this policy, people change careers, lifestyles, homes, states they live in, and put new life into their marriages. Past decisions that haven't worked for both parties can be renegotiated. They can bring back that compatibility that brought them together in the first place.

Goals of marriage. Marriages can benefit from an attitude of couples committing themselves to being each other's greatest source of happiness. They meet each other's most important emotional needs. If they do that, wonderful things will happen in the marriage that will take care of most of the unpleasantness between them.

Couples need to avoid being each other's greatest source of unhappiness. In Harley's estimation, 20 to 30 percent of marriages need to clean up the anger, disrespect, criticisms, demands and dishonesty that take away the feelings of love even when important emotional needs are being met.

Becoming an expert on meeting a spouse's emotional needs and avoiding being the source of your spouse's greatest unhappiness are two keys to a good marriage.

JEALOUSY CAN PUSH A SPOUSE AWAY
CHAPTER FIFTY

How can a hard working, steady, generally level-headed man lose his cool and become irrational and obsessed to the point of driving away someone he loves? Meet Bill and Nora - not their real names, of course.

Bill is a reserved man, a bedrock of strength and virtue. He is loyal and dedicated, a plodding man who advanced in his company through sheer effort and determination. He had an abusive childhood he doesn't talk much about and when he does, he minimizes any psychological impact on his life.

Nora's personality is the opposite of Bill's. Nora has an easy way with people. She is exuberant, fun loving, and wears her emotions on her sleeve. Her joy of life is contagious. She has a lot of friends, whether it is at work, in her church circle or socially. Bill is reminded of this at social gatherings when Nora displays a magnetic effect on others.

Bill becomes jealous by how Nora acts in public. If fact, if he had his way, they wouldn't go out much at all. When they do go out, Bill invariably gets into a dark, ugly mood. He wants some of the attention she gives to others. He feels slighted. He finds fault with Nora's friendliness and gives her the third degree about her actions and conversations.

Nora doesn't think twice about her motives. She resents having to explain her innocent behavior. Bill's accusations are groundless and absurd. She resents the implication that her morals are suspect or that she is gullible. Nora's attempts to reassure Bill don't stop his jealousy. Simple occasions have the potential for disaster - either on the spot or after they go home.

Bill's active imagination almost seems like paranoia. He now starts interrogating Nora about her conversations with male friends at church meetings and keeps track of how long she takes to get home.

Nora resents his control and chooses to defy him. She goes out with her friends just to prove she has the right to do so. To avoid unpleasant clashes, Nora withholds information or tells a few "white lies." This backfires. When Bill "catches" her, his worst fears are confirmed and the pressure intensifies. This panics Nora even more. He is wearing her out with his endless accusations and questions.

Nora becomes depressed. She can't go on this way. She's losing her love for Bill. The man she counted on for stability and good judgment is falling apart. She starts threatening to leave him if wild accusations continue. Bringing up separation or divorce triggers even more of Bill's insecurities. Ironically, Bill has caused the thing he fears most - losing Nora.

Jealousy stems from poor self-esteem. At the heart of jealousy is a crisis of self-esteem. Nora's effervescent personality and smooth social skills are quite a contrast to Bill's reserved, introverted manner. He began to believe she was too perfect, too good and that he was unworthy to have her. Worse, he imagined that she would recognize this and be attracted to someone else.

Since Bill didn't trust his hold on Nora's love, he became obsessed with keeping potential rivals out of her life. His suspicious interrogations, wild accusations, and rigid control were efforts to fend off threatening relationships before they could get started. He treated Nora like a possession he was going to keep at all costs.

What Bill feared happened. Nora pulled away. He can't make the connection that it was his control and jealousy that drove Nora away. He was too fixated on what she was doing wrong.

Advice for Bill. Bill has forgotten how well he and Nora were matched up emotionally, spiritually, and intellectually. Nora saw in Bill qualities she admired, respected, and loved. His strength and steadiness appealed to her. How he was then and how he is now --

minus the jealousy -- met Nora's needs. Bill has to reaffirm his trust of his own desirability; something Nora believes more than he does. Nora pins her hopes on getting in for professional counseling.

Bill's self-confidence is a key to letting go of his fears. He needs an attitude that Nora is just as lucky to be with him as he is to be with her. It was that independence and self-assurance that drew Nora to him in the first place. Bill is worrying too much about himself and his needs. Besides his fears, his obsession about himself and his feelings have become the problem. Can he get back to caring about her instead of worrying about himself?

Bill needs to refocus his attention on meeting Nora's needs. He needs to lighten up, listen to her feelings, and go out of his way for her in a non-smothering way. Their relationship needs some lighthearted fun instead of a suffocating atmosphere of conflict and control.

Nora needs freedom and trust. Bill can get her heart back only by letting go. No amount of force or pressure will keep her. Nora already loves him -- the way he used to be. By relaxing and believing and then admitting he is the problem, Bill can get back to being himself - the self that won Nora's heart in the first place.

DO YOUR LOVE STORIES MATCH?
CHAPTER FIFTY-ONE

Alise feels that a loving relationship should be smooth, tranquil and relatively conflict-free. She believes that if two people love each other, they should accept each other as they are. She avoids arguments and confrontations with her husband, Zach.

On the other hand, what Alise thinks are verbal attacks, Zach calls discussions. He believes that a couple should confront their differences, solve problems and forge a common path. He is quick to confront Alise when he sees problems.

Alise perceives confrontations as attacks - exactly what two people who love each other should not do. She withdraws. Zach becomes more aggressive in his attempt to bring out problems. This results in Alise withdrawing even further. Their relationship gets worse.

What is going wrong here? This couple sees the facts about the same. They love each other. What is wrong is that they have different stories about what love is all about. That leads them to interpret events in opposite ways.

How Zach and Alise feel about their relationship depends on how well it matches up with their expectations of what love should be like. Zach and Alise don't understand each other's story about love, nor do they understand their own very well. These stories come from childhood, from observing their parents' marriages, and from peer relationships, media, religious values and culture.

Love stories generally fit with what culture says about true love. The love story competes with other stories about careers and family life. The love story is embedded within the context of other unfolding dramas of life.

A perfect match - infatuation. A romantic partner experiences a surge of emotion or infatuation when he or she matches up with a person who is close to his or her ideal love story. If the dating partner is a close match, then imagination takes over and transforms the person into an ideal match. Actions are interpreted with rose colored glasses.

Often, the ideal partner has many attributes that are lacking or longed for in oneself. After the honeymoon, reality sets in. The differences between the ideal and actual partner become obvious. Instead of feeling deprived of an ideal partner, the challenge is to change his or her love story to fit the relationship as it actually is.

A history of rejection. Suppose Zach has a history of feeling rejected, feeling unloved or unworthy of love. He is likely to be highly sensitive to rejection and to interpret Alise's behavior of withdrawing as rejection, even if it wasn't intended that way. Rejection is likely to become a major theme of Zach's love story, woven into every plot.

With a history of mistrusting loved ones, Zach would be looking for signs that Alise is not worthy of trust. Zach would be vigilant in looking for themes of deception and would weave them into his story. Once a story is created, Zach will continue the story in a consistent way. Nobody likes reading a novel that blatantly contradicts itself. New events are interpreted so they make sense with what happened previously. He invents what is not there. He rewrites history to match his story.

Alise ignores inconsistent information as long as possible to avoid change. Their relationship gets into big trouble when Alise figures out that her story is no longer the way she wants it to be. Zach's insecurities are no longer interpreted as devotion and adoration but as jealousy, possessiveness and control. What used to be flattering becomes annoying. Behavior that was tolerated before is no longer tolerated. Her love story doesn't include mistrust and accusations.

It is hard to give up part of an ideal story or to admit that the love story has a fatal flaw. Love stories are not right or wrong. Something has to give. Behavior needs to match the stories or the stories need to be altered to fit the behavior.

Alise then creates reasons for wanting a divorce just like she created reasons for getting married. The reasons are justification to herself and others on why she is doing what she is doing. The real reason for their breakup it that she feels the love story she is living has turned into a bad story, a story that she doesn't like.

Happily ever after. Until the story changes, the relationship cannot change. A new love story might save a relationship. The plot takes a twist to include going to counseling. A chapter is added on how Zach learns to understand where his insecurities came from, to trust Alise's love, and to understand her withdrawal as her distrust of conflict - not rejection. Alise's love story might change to include how love includes more togetherness and how working through conflict can draw them closer together.

With the help of a counselor, they replot their story to fit the changes they need to make their love story work. Love stories can be changed. Zach and Alise are both authors in their own personal love story and can change it to whatever they want. The challenge is to write a happy ending.

This story is based on ideas from psychologist Robert J. Sternberg of Yale University.

DON'T FIGHT FIRE WITH FIRE - OR ICE
CHAPTER FIFTY-TWO

Fire. Half of all divorces occur in the first seven years of marriage. Sparks of white hot conflict, scathing sarcasm and caustic criticism are the incendiary fuel that doom relationships lacking in impulse control and problem-solving skills. These couples attack and defend with escalating anger and conflict. Their explosive interactions leave one or both partners feeling disheartened and overwhelmed by negative feelings. That is the fire.

Ice. But what about ice? A second vulnerable period for divorce occurs in midlife when teens are in the home or when they are leaving the nest. These troubled marriages are characterized by emotional coolness and suppression of feelings.

These couples don't talk a lot. They don't fight a lot. They no longer raise issues. There is an undercurrent of hostility about disappointed expectations and past failed efforts to create change. There is no joy, no fun, no expression of positive emotion. They are resigned to an intense loneliness that almost feels like dying. Long-standing unexpressed disillusionment about the marriage is amplified by serious thoughts about aging and the loss of opportunity for personal happiness.

This delicate equilibrium is upset when one spouse, usually the one who is most unhappy, goes underground with his or her feelings and forms an alliance with a teenage son or daughter of the same gender. It then becomes two against one. Getting a teenager into the fray creates enough conflict that the situation reaches a threshold of distress and open conflict.

The situation becomes worse when the one spouse, usually the wife, tries to get her husband to enter counseling and he refuses. She then goes for individual counseling, forms an alliance with the therapist and gets validation for her marital unhappiness. The pattern of emotional withdrawal continues its destructive course.

Types of withdrawal. How does this downward cycle of avoidance and withdrawal get started? Researcher Linda Roberts of the University of Wisconsin-Madison published her findings in the Journal of Marriage and the Family. She identified and assessed three distinct types of withdrawal behavior:

- *Angry withdrawal*, occurring in response to perceived negative behavior of a partner and expressed through actions such as stomping out of the room, pouting or giving the silent treatment.

- *Conflict avoidance*, occurring in response to conflict or a potential conflict, with a partner. This is expressed through actions such as changing the subject, making a joke, placating, failing to bring up a disagreement or demonstrating a lack of interest in a discussion.

- *Intimacy avoidance*, occurring in response to a partner's self-revealing disclosures of feelings and vulnerabilities, and expressed through behaviors such as ignoring, showing a lack of attention or interest, or not listening.

Roberts found that patterns of avoidance of intimacy - particularly withdrawal from situations requiring emotional closeness, warmth and caring - are destructive to marital happiness.

Gender differences. Roberts also found gender differences in how husbands and wives react to emotional withdrawal. Conflict avoidance may be positive for some couples and negative for others.

Wives react positively to a husband's conflict-avoiding behaviors if the alternative is hostile responsiveness. On the other hand, wives who perceive their husbands as unlikely to blow up and be hostile in response to conflict, react negatively when their husbands avoid conflict.

Of the two, a wife's distress is most affected by hostile negativity, more so than withdrawal. Husbands who see their wives as withdrawing emotionally are more unhappy than those husbands who see their wives as hostile and critical.

Breaking the cycle. It is particularly important to wives that negative feelings are aired and conflicts resolved in a context that feels safe and constructive. It is important to husbands that their wives are engaged, involved and responsive to their communications.

In either case, it is important that both partners are responsive to their spouse's disclosure of personal, heartfelt feelings. They need to listen to each other and respond with empathy, interest and concern. They can establish the pattern of talking by greeting one another, sharing the details of each other's lives - their dreams, hopes, fears and disappointments early in the marriage - and by not allowing emotional distance to come between them.

If couples have fallen into a trap of busyness or the pursuit of individual goals, they can try to break through the walls that have come up and get to know their spouse again. It may take counseling, showing empathy for each other's concerns, working through past anger and hurts, and a willingness to stop avoiding the difficult differences that place an icy pall over their marriage. Couples disconnected in midlife can use their unhappiness as a bridge to find one another again instead of letting their loneliness take them out of the marriage.

"Overall, the results (of the research) send a strong message about the importance of staying involved with your spouse, listening to his or her concerns, and responding in a non-hostile and caring way," says Roberts. *"Spouses shouldn't fight fire with fire - or with ice."*

Part X: Protecting Your Marriage From An Affair

I didn't marry you because you were perfect. I didn't even marry you because I loved you. I married you because you gave me a promise. That promise made up for your faults. And the promise I gave you made up for mine. Two imperfect people got married and it was the promise that made the marriage. And when our children were growing up, it wasn't a house that protected them, and it wasn't our love that protected them - it was that promise.
- Thornton Wilder

LOYALTY IS A TEST OF LOVE
CHAPTER FIFTY-THREE

It is possible to love two people at the same time. I see it all the time in my counseling office when people describe their affairs. They love their spouse and they love their affair partner. They are paralyzed with indecision because they love both individuals. The love they feel is a function of getting to know two people too well. Both their spouse and their affair partner are loveable, admirable, and are completely capable of giving and sharing love.

You can love two people at the same time - not in the same way and for different reasons - but you can only give loyalty to one. That's where the ethics and morality of decisions come in. For morality's sake and for peace of mind, don't try it. Loving two people at the same time can "eat you alive." It is painful and it comes to an unhappy consequence with major betrayal and personal anguish.

People have to guard against affairs by watching the quality of their cross-sex friendships. Deliberately avoid the type of intimate conversations that would lead to a compassionate, loving relationship with a "friend" that might set up a competing love and trigger impulses toward more intimacy - including physical intimacy.

By having two relationships at once, the lover chooses to be loyal to one partner by keeping the relationship a secret, or by sharing information about one relationship with the other but not visa versa. It is the "insider" who gets the loyalty.

True loyalty isn't tested until the lover has to make a final choice between the two parties. He or she has to give up one love over the other because divided loyalties destroy trust in both relationships. Loving two people at the same time does emotional violence to the betrayed party to whom the original commitment was made.

Feelings follow loyalty. While the affair is going on, generally the offender redefines what is happening in their marriage as not true love, or maybe was never true love, to justify his or her behavior. The offender rejects or withdraws from his or her marital partner because of the loyalty issue. Feelings of not being in love happen *after* behavior such as disloyalty or beliefs about absent or flawed love occur. People rewrite the history of their courtship and marriage to account for their disloyal behavior.

By eliminating the association with the affair partner and by redefining that relationship as less than true love, the offender then can "feel" love for his or her spouse again. If an offender defines the feelings toward the affair partner as an infatuation or something less than true love, then it is easier to give up the relationship.

In the case of an affair partner, there is usually evidence to substantiate the fact that it is not true love because the lovers are sharing only a portion of their life together and were deceitful to themselves and others to justify what they were doing.

Love is a choice. Love is behavior. Love is consistent loving behavior - sustained attention and concern over time. Feelings are a part of love, but feelings follow the way we behave - if for no other reason than to reduce cognitive dissonance. Conversely, behavior doesn't necessarily follow feelings. If it did, this would be one heck of an undisciplined and impulsive world. It is hard to change feelings unless there is also behavioral change.

"Real" love encompasses loyalty. Choosing to have a competing love in your life is a violent disservice and betrayal to one or both of the partners. One relationship might have primacy over the other or alternate depending on the circumstances. In a behavioral way, love is being withheld from either the affair partner or the spouse. For love to be sustained, love needs to be loyal.

Having two romantic attachments at once is not pleasant. It is painful or will become painful. It means eventually having to give up one of the parties and, in the meantime, living with competing loyalties. For those who have been there, it is a terrible place to be. Deceit and disloyalty are tough to live with. Wanting both relationships and knowing that it is impossible is a fence nobody wants to be on.

Stay away. Loyalty and honoring commitments are a test of love. People can retain full consciousness of their feelings of love toward their affair partner and choose not to act on them. When I tell a person who has violated their marital vows by infidelity to categorically stay away from their affair partner, I am doing it to allow time for the feelings to diminish. This takes time. Staying away represents a choice - which is an act of love toward the person you are now choosing to love.

The betrayed spouse shouldn't be too alarmed by residual feelings their marital partner may have for the affair partner as long as there is no contact between them. The choice has been made. Feelings will diminish. What needs to happen now is an outpouring of love, concern and unselfish behavior. As time passes, these loving actions coupled with efforts the offender puts forth to make amends become trusted and real.

Can we love more than one person at a time? Yes, if we allow ourselves to. But we can't be loyal to both.

OPPOSITE SEX FRIENDSHIPS ARE A THREAT TO MARRIAGE
CHAPTER FIFTY-FOUR

Can married partners have cross-sex friendships that are rewarding and yet not threaten the quality of their marital relationship? Does friendship necessarily turn into passion? Supposing both friends felt that there was no sexual tension between them, would there still be a problem?

Before considering the ways opposite sex friendships can be a danger to marriage, here are some points that proponents of cross-sex friendships mention when defending the practice:

- Everything in life isn't sex-motivated. There are relationships where there is no spark, no attraction, no sexual friction. These relationships offer a window to the male or female psyche in the absence of sexual tension. "He is the 'big brother' I've always dreamed of having."

- Advice and viewpoints from the opposite sex can be enlightening, especially when the friend doesn't have a stake in the outcome. Friendship, respect and a certain level of intimacy can grow with colleagues in the workplace without damaging primary relations at home.

- We can experience freedom and playfulness in a safe relationship where there is no control or possessiveness to complicate the relationship. Opposite sex friendships offer an avenue for needed emotional and social acceptance.

- Opposite sex friendships affirm our masculine and feminine qualities. These relationships have the quality of innocent flirting . . . of making people feel good about themselves. It reinforces the feeling that members of the opposite sex find us interesting and attractive.

- Even if we experience some sexual tension in the relationship, we do not have to act on it. We have the self-discipline and inner values to recognize appropriate and inappropriate behavior and not to step over the line. Married men and women deal with this all the time. There are unspoken rules for being intimate without getting intimate.

- Not all needs can be met by one person. Having cross-sex friendships reduces the amount of expectations on the marriage. "I like women, talking to them, being fascinated by them. Each woman has something different to offer." Extra-marital friendships can enrich a marriage.

Why opposite sex friendships are a threat to marriage. Many people stumble into affairs that begin with simple opposite sex friendships. These friendships can be justified as innocent because there is a lack of sexual attraction. Advice and outlook from the opposite sex can be enlightening and helpful.

Husbands and wives are so sure of their ability to honor their vows of sexual fidelity that they don't recognize the dangers associated with opposite sex friendships. Here are seven cautionary points to consider in evaluating how these friendships may weaken and destroy a marriage.

1. Emotional intimacy can lead to physical intimacy. Rarely are opposite sex friendships emotionally pure. Sexual tension is always present, whether it is acted on or not. That's what makes it interesting.

Affairs have innocent beginnings. Opposite sex friends may work hard to deny the erotic sparks. Sexual attraction may not surface until the level of emotional intimacy has progressed to deeper levels. As you come to know and admire someone, your feelings of closeness may mature into creating that spark of erotic interest that wasn't there in the beginning. "His admiration triggered a response in me." Friendships can evolve into passion as well as the other way around.

The natural conclusion to conversational intimacy is physical intimacy. A natural progression of intimacy is a desire to touch or physically draw close to your friend. Non-sexual hugs and touches lead to intimate touch until the relationship is consummated with sexual relations. Affairs often begin as slow but evolving friendships.

2. Vulnerability or openness to an affair can change with circumstances. What may be safe now may not be safe later when there are serious misunderstandings, conflict or pressures on you or your marriage. There are ups and downs to every relationship. During a time of vulnerability, the comfort and acceptance of the special friend may appear in a different light. What was formerly inconceivable intrudes into one's imagination.

Rationalizations begin. Strong values are compromised. Suppressed feelings become actions. Affairs begin when we know or admire someone too well or when we begin to confide about problems in our marriage. Affairs have innocent beginnings in friendships.

3. Secrecy is disloyalty. If there is self-consciousness about not revealing the friendship or any conversations or meetings with your friend to your spouse, you have already crossed a line of disloyalty. Lies can destroy trust, the foundation of a marriage. If your spouse can keep something like this from you, what else is there? Any secretive friendship can be labeled an emotional affair.

4. Comparisons weaken marriage. The perception of positive qualities in a friend might lead to feelings of deprivation within the marriage. By contrast, our spouse doesn't excite us like the friend. Comparisons are inevitable. Our admiration and appreciation of our friend may lead to a subtle dissatisfaction with certain qualities in our spouse.

It is a false comparison. Spouses live in the real world where they have commitments and responsibilities. It isn't always possible to have "on demand" intimacy or attention.

Friendships are generally devoid of problems and differences to work out. Differences are real and exist between any couple. Confiding in a friend can be a substitute for working through problems with a spouse.

When we take off our rose-colored glasses, we begin to find fault or criticize behavior that we formerly overlooked as charming or mildly exasperating. This turns to feelings of dissatisfaction, deprivation and unhappiness. Opposite sex friendships don't have a future. Marriage does. Opposite sex friendships don't have problems to work out. Marriage does.

5. Marriage needs emotional intimacy. We have limited time and energy to spend on relationships. Emotional closeness and sharing in friendships takes away energy, ideas and closeness from the marriage. These needs are being met elsewhere.

The friendship represents an intrusion into the private world of the couple. Certain conversations are special, saved only for the partner. You can be disloyal with the heart, not only with the body. A married couple shares a privately defined view of the world that is meant for them and them only.

Sexual identity and identity are close to being one and the same, the essence of who we are. Sharing special feelings, playfulness, dreams, joys, despair, hurts and trials is sharing your masculinity and femininity in ways that should be reserved for your partner and your partner alone. This "soul-matching" outside of marriage robs the possibilities of these magical moments of bonding from happening inside the marriage.

6. Sharing marriage problems or providing a listening ear is dangerous. Conversations about marital problems with an opposite sex friend is being disloyal and provides fertile ground for getting needed compassion, comfort and understanding. This lays the groundwork for an affair. The friendship provides a sharp contrast in understanding and is already an act of disloyalty. The friend has replaced your spouse as your true confidant and "insider" in your life.

As a friend, when you provide compassionate listening to a troubled spouse, you may awaken or create feelings in yourself or in your friend that go far beyond simple help. Be ready to avoid these types of conversations and refer your friend to clergy, mental health professionals, counselors, family members, and or a same sex friend for the advice or help he or she needs.

7. Opposite sex friendships can threaten a spouse's sense of security. The power and attraction of the friendship makes the spouse feel inadequate and insecure. He or she might wonder, "What am I not doing or bringing to the marriage? What is wrong with me? Why does my partner have the freedom to speak with a friend in a way that doesn't happen between us?"

For the sake of the marriage, why take any risks with friendships that potentially could detract from marital trust and security? If you have no other reason, protecting your partner's sense of security and well-being should be reason enough to curtail these kinds of friendships.

Are opposite sex friendships a threat to marriage? What do you think?

WHY GOOD PEOPLE CHEAT
ON THEIR SPOUSES
CHAPTER FIFTY-FIVE

I once did a column on fraud, embezzlement and white collar crime. I interviewed Tom Buckhoff, PhD, CPA, Certified Fraud Examiner, and faculty member at Georgia State University. He specializes in fraud detection, investigation and prevention.

He explained a theory from his field that I think has application to understand why good people with high moral standards cheat on their spouses. Buckhoff describes three basic elements necessary for fraud to occur - opportunity, pressure, and rationalization of values.

Opportunity. Opportunity can be real or perceived. Opportunity comes with poor or nonexistent controls with a person who is in a key position of trust within the organization. The most common comment Buckhoff hears from owners, managers or partners is, "I can't believe he would do this. He was my most trusted employee."

People are able to commit fraud precisely because they are trusted. People who think they will be detected rarely commit fraud. In a world of men and women in the workplace, personal mobility, business and professional travel, and socializing among friends, opportunities for affairs exist.

There are danger points in opposite gender relationships: intimate conversations, confiding about or listening to marital problems, and flirtatious behavior that suggests opportunity. Husbands and wives can prevent affairs by avoiding these kind of "innocent" beginnings that mushroom into real opportunity.

Vigilance, surveillance, and interrogations might reduce the opportunity for an affair to occur. However, this is counterproductive to a good relationship. Relationships work best when there is trust and the control is internal.

Pressure. The right amount of pressure can cause even honest people to commit fraud. Employees under a lot of pressure should not be exposed to positions of financial temptation. Examples of pressure include: living extravagantly beyond one's means, having personal debt, alcohol, drug or gambling addictions, or job dissatisfaction.

In marital relationships, what are the internal pressures that condition people for affairs? Maybe it is marital dissatisfaction based on the lack of emotional needs being met, solved or even discussed. Perhaps it is high conflict and poor problem-solving that takes a toll on emotional and physical intimacy. Perhaps there are sexual problems and dissatisfaction.

It could be all kinds of things. The point is, marriage takes work. There are ups and downs to any relationship and strong and weak points in any partner. Fidelity is not based on feeling love or happiness all the time.

When there is unhappiness in marriage, it needs to be addressed through heart-to-heart discussion and, if one's best efforts fail, marital counseling. By living in a persistently unhappy condition, you become vulnerable to an affair. Partners need to know about the emotional details of their spouse's life and to respond to complaints and concerns as they come up.

Rationalization. The third element for fraud to occur is the ability to rationalize one's behavior. A person committing fraud needs to rationalize the fraud so the fraudulent activities are consistent with his/her personal code of conduct. A disgruntled employee can rationalize that he or she is overworked, underpaid or unappreciated. Theft can be perceived as a way of getting justice or retaliation.

To live with one's self a person has to explain his or her fraud as OK, that what he or she is doing isn't that wrong. Someone who is prone to excuse making or not taking responsibility for mistakes finds it easier to rationalize the personal use of business resources.

Here are some other common rationalizations. "I'm only borrowing the money. I'll pay it back." "Everyone does it." "I'm not hurting anyone." "It's for a good purpose." "It's not that serious."

In the world of affairs, what are some common rationalizations? "We are just friends." "How could something that makes me feel good and loved be wrong?" "I don't have feelings for my spouse anymore." "I deserve love." "She will never know about this." "Our marriage is over anyway." "I will never leave my wife and family - this is something that will end and no one needs to know."

One justification leads to another and soon the wayward spouse is on a slippery slope. It is a short distance from a secretive meeting or an after work conversation to a first kiss. It is a short distance from a first kiss to sexual intimacy. The self-deception, lies and deception start right from the beginning as the offender explores a "real" opportunity for an affair.

The combination. The combination of all three factors, opportunity, pressure, and ability to rationalize, come together in a way that people with good values are caught up in illicit behavior. Sometimes people are faithful because there is no real opportunity to be unfaithful. Sometimes people are faithful because they are happy and content with their lives, especially with their marriage. This won't always be the case.

What is the best way to protect your marriage from affairs? It is the ability to honor one's vows no matter what. It is knowing that adultery is wrong, that it destroys trust and inflicts great harm. It is your moral and religious values and beliefs that underpin character and trust. That is what your spouse needs to count on.

Having an affair depends on three elements: opportunity, pressure, and ability to rationalize. There will be opportunities. The pressures of life will occasionally make us vulnerable. Our true protection lies in our values, loyalty, honesty and honor. Knowing who we are and what we stand for is our protection from being able to rationalize an affair.

THERE IS NO SUCH THING AS AN ACCIDENTAL AFFAIR

CHAPTER FIFTY-SIX

Want to ruin a perfectly good marriage and family? Not likely. Yet many well meaning people with good character put their marriages in jeopardy by having an affair. They put their marriage at risk by crossing over important boundaries meant to protect marriage.

Honorable people dishonor themselves and engage in lies, deceit and betrayal. Marital vows go by the wayside. Great trauma is inflicted upon the innocent spouse. Also, if great effort and humility aren't put forth to repair the harm, innocent children and an innocent spouse suffer the maelstrom of divorce.

Unfortunately, our culture and our media are not helpful. Our consumer culture glamorizes and objectifies sex, reducing it to a physical act devoid of meaning and unrelated to commitment and family life. Sex is treated like a commodity. Sex is used to sell tickets and merchandise. If our personal experience doesn't measure up to the hype, the fantasies and the unrealistic importance our culture puts on sex, then we feel deprived.

Movies and television portray romance between unmarried partners and between extra-marital partners as love or the awkward beginnings of love. Romance isn't love. Under the right circumstances it can lead to love. The romance of Hollywood is more about self-delusion, excitement, infatuation, and narcissistic fantasies – another bill of goods that doesn't measure up to the emotional freight of happiness it is supposed to carry.

Love isn't a feeling. Love is behavior. Love is based on honor, respect, trust, deep sharing, friendship, and acts of love and consideration invested on a daily basis.

We are also led to believe that infidelity is caused by imperfect marriages. Wrong! All marriages have their imperfections, moods, and rough spots. Lots of happily married partners have affairs and lots of unhappily married partners don't. Marital problems are a rationalization for an affair.

People can address martital unhappiness in a lot of other ways besides having an affair. An affair becomes the biggest marital problem and immensely complicates finding the solutions to any pre-existing difficulties. An affair makes your marriage partner an outsider and breaks down intimacy at all levels.

Affairs are preventable. Here are some common sense guidelines for protecting your marriage from the heartbreak and trauma of an affair.

You can be unfaithful without intercourse. An emotional affair can be just as devastating to a marriage as a physical one. People slide into affairs by getting to know someone too well, usually in the workplace. It starts with intimate conversation. You can love more than one person at a time, if you get to know them well enough.

Be careful of "just friends." It is not just friends. At least not for long. Some of the elements of an affair are secrecy, emotional intimacy and sexual attraction. The first sign of danger that important boundaries are being crossed is when you begin to lie or hide the relationship. Share your friendships with your spouse present.

Don't discuss marriage problems with a sympathetic, receptive and caring person from the other gender. That kind of communication should be with same sex friends, relatives or within the safety of professional counseling. Many affairs get started as people commiserate with each other. The emotional intimacy created by good listening is powerful and contrasts favorably with the marriage.

Watch out for old flames, especially first lovers. Don't set up secret meetings. Invite your spouse along.

The Internet is dangerous. It has the potential for intimacy, secrecy, and sexual banter/arousal. Beware of chat rooms. Show your spouse all your e-mails. Secrecy around any relationship gives it power. Pornography can fuel marital dissatisfaction and infidelity.

Be careful about relationships with opposite sex guests in the home. The home is a powerful, intimate setting. When coupled with intimate conversations, the opportunity for an affair increases.

Attraction is normal. Flirting is dangerous. There are points in any marriage when you are vulnerable. Harmless flirting suddenly isn't so harmless. Flirting creates fantasy and fantasy precedes an affair. It is dangerous to fantasize about real people in your life. Saying "yes" to an affair happens in the head before it happens in real life. There is a thought process that takes place before an affair. Being aware of fantasies will give you early warning to stop a relationship before it gets started.

Watch who you choose for friends, colleagues, and role models. How do your associates handle their marriage vows? It becomes easier to rationalize your behavior when people you admire and enjoy being with are unfaithful. The so-called innocent "boys night out" or "girls night out" is a dangerous path to walk.

There is no excuse for an affair. None. You don't have to take the first steps that place you on that slippery slope.

Part XI: Apologies And Forgiveness

*To heal, you need to forgive, but your partner
must apply salve to your wounds first.
- Janis Abrams Spring*

PUTTING THE PAST IN THE PAST
CHAPTER FIFTY-SEVEN

Not far down the list of marital complaints in a counselor's office is "bringing up the past." Past hurts, trauma, resentments, anger and unresolved problems bubble to the surface like flotsam on a backwater pond.

No resolution of the event. Every marriage has its history of stupidity, willful misconduct, selfish acts, neglect, betrayal or even cruelty. One act can be remembered because of its powerful effect. The wound was grievous and not enough was done to rectify the harm caused.

The hurtful event hasn't been repeated. Everything that can be learned from the incident has been learned and there is no value in discussing it further. It won't happen again. The connection to a current problem is vague or non-existent, yet the pain and bad memories continue to fester. The issue lies there, like so many other weeds in a garden, growing and eventually choking off the fruit and the flower of the marriage.

Past is still present. When actions are repeated and destructive habits go uncorrected over time, good feelings are drained out of marriage. Promises are made but not kept. Attempts to change fail. The past isn't left in the past because the problems are as current as today's newspaper.

If there is a perceived connection between past hurts and a

current problem, then the past becomes a legitimate example of how the problem is continuing. By objecting to a discussion of the past, the repeat offender either doesn't "get it" or is trying to deny or obscure the connection. Complaining about bringing up the past can be a ploy for avoiding the fact that a harmful pattern of behavior hasn't been stopped.

Offender has to do more. The negative emotions and memory won't go away because of the lack of acknowledgment of the harm that was caused and the lack of a heartfelt plea for forgiveness. Victims of trauma need this to move forward.

I've seen too many instances where the hurt was swept under the rug, ignored and left unacknowledged. It won't go away until a proper apology has been made. The lack of an apology may be the only thing preventing the past from being put in the past. I've seen instant relief and equally quick forgiveness once a genuine apology has been given.

Why are people reluctant to apologize? Why don't they say the words that need to be said to repair the harm they caused? I suppose pride has something to do with it. Maybe they don't understand how important an apology is in the healing process.

Feeling bad and not repeating the problem are not enough. Justice demands confession and restitution. To the extent that he or she can, an offender has to make amends for the harm caused. The failure to put forth effort to make amends can often be a stumbling block to the process of letting go of the past.

The past as a weapon. Sometimes the past is unfairly brought up as a weapon, or as a powerful distracter when one is losing an argument. It is painful. Unfortunately, it works.

However, if the relevance to the topic at hand isn't made, the recipient feels helpless and ambushed by an unfair fight. It feels like a sledgehammer has been brought out to smash a mosquito. Retaliation is not possible.

Failure to forgive. If appropriate acknowledgment, apologies and amends are made, the burden then shifts to the victim to forgive. The failure to forgive may cause equal or greater harm to the marriage than the actual act itself. In a similar manner to how unexpressed apologies keep the past alive, unexpressed forgiveness holds the offender captive and withholds a final resolution of the problem.

Forgiveness means letting go. It means giving up the power of victimhood and turning a new page in the marriage. It means accepting that justice-- however meager and unequal to the original harm-- has been meted out. That's the best it will ever be. It is time to move on. Saying the words of forgiveness is as important as saying the actual apology. It is a clear signal that the past is over. Too many times the failure to say, "I forgive you," keeps the past alive.

For a full restoration of a relationship, offenders have to acknowledge the harm, apologize and make amends. They must first make a commitment not to repeat the offending action and second live up to the commitments they have made.

GUILT WARNS US TO CORRECT RELATIONSHIP PROBLEMS
CHAPTER FIFTY-EIGHT

Is guilt good or bad? Is guilt a private emotion that wells up when we violate a personal standard of conduct? Or does guilt also serve a purpose in maintaining important social bonds?

A violation of standards. The traditional definition of guilt is defined as an emotion that alerts us to when our actions have fallen short of our moral standards of conduct.

These standards of conduct are derived from social norms or affiliation. Guilt involves the relationship between an individual and a group. The feeling of belonging or being in harmony to a valued group such as a culture, religion or organization is part of our personal identity and well-being.

When an individual violates standards of performance related to the group, guilt is an inducement to take corrective action so that one's position with the group isn't at stake. Guilt can be seen as a social emotion because it is an early warning signal that personal behavior has to be brought in line with group standards.

Keeping social bonds. Psychologist Roy Baumeister at Florida State University finds that guilt is primarily a social emotion that helps maintain strong, close relationships. He believes that guilt comes when we sense that we have caused distress and suffering to someone who is close to us. It is our ability to empathize with others in our lives that alerts us to their pain and distress.

People make changes in their lives when they truly perceive the pain they have caused. One pathway to rehabilitation for criminal offenders is for them to meet with the victims, listen to them and fully appreciate the harm that has been done.

Loss of relationship. Another cause of guilt stems from anxiety over a possible loss of a relationship. The main cause of guilt is the awareness that the offender has done something that has hurt someone close to them. If the offending actions are repeated often enough or severely enough, they may eventually cause the partner to break off the relationship.

The threat of losing the relationship triggers a fear of rejection or abandonment. Guilt is an early warning signal that, if persisted in, further offending actions are likely to be hazardous to the bond or connection. Guilt serves a useful purpose to protect, preserve and enhance good relationships.

Ways guilt helps. Baumeister identifies three ways guilt corrects relationships and keeps them on a positive course.

1. Guilt is an unpleasant emotion. People avoid doing things to avoid feeling guilty. Guilt induces needed changes that benefit and strengthen the relationship. In Baumeister's research, he found the single biggest thing people feel guilty about is not paying enough attention to someone.

If people respond to guilt, they will give more attention to their relationship partners. The guilty party can get back into good graces with the offended partner by changing his or her behavior.

Other actions to restore the relationship might include apologizing, confessing the transgression, making amends where possible, making commitments for change and becoming more loving and helpful. Guilt has done its job if important lessons have been learned and behavior is changed.

2. Guilt helps people create change without using power or coercion. If the offended partner in a relationship induces guilt through the obvious hurt and suffering, the other party may change his or her behavior.

The less powerful partner in a relationship can influence the more powerful partner and correct the imbalance of power by saying, "Look how you are hurting me." The offender understands what he or she is doing and shows compassion for the partner.

3. The transgressor in a relationship has benefited in some way. Guilt is caused as a result of neglect, unfulfilled obligations or selfish actions. Guilt transfers the bad feelings from the victim to the transgressor. "Guilt is the very nerve of sorrow."

When the transgressor feels sorrow and guilt, the victim feels better. This brings the two parties into closer harmony because they are reacting emotionally in similar ways.

If guilt is so good, should we induce it? Inducing guilt as a strategy for correcting a relationship can be costly. The other party may not feel he or she is responsible for hurt feelings. Attempts to induce guilt can come across as manipulation or control.

There are other ways of equalizing power in a relationship. When the offense is obvious, the guilt needed to trigger the change will occur without inducement. When your partner isn't clear about the offense, inducing guilt could backfire. Resentment is possible either way - whether the guilt is deserved or undeserved.

The issue might be better handled through direct requests for change, negotiations and communications. Requests for change becomes the part of a normal relationship of give and take. In some cases, this might be better for the relationship.

Some people feel guilty about inducing guilt. It doesn't feel good. For them, there are better ways to correct the relationship.

Is guilt good? Guilt is unpleasant but quite useful. The negative emotions are painful but doing something about guilty feelings can change a negative emotion into a positive one. Late warnings or no warnings that the relationship is in jeopardy would be much more painful.

WHEN YOUR PARTNER WASN'T THERE FOR YOU

CHAPTER FIFTY-NINE

One vital dimension of marriage is that it provides the sense of security we need to face the major problems of life. It is like having someone in your corner when life gets overwhelming - someone you can turn to for comfort and support.

The need for a strong marriage in today's society is becoming magnified because of the loss of community and family supports. Being lonely and alone is more dangerous to mortality than smoking. A dependable source of intimacy is an essential buffer for dealing with stress and trauma.

People count on their spouse to care, soothe and comfort them, especially during times of crisis. It is part of the bargain of marriage. Even if there are differences and conflicts in a marriage, what makes the relationship secure is the ability of the couple to stay connected emotionally and to be able to retreat to one another's arms for comfort and care.

Attachment bond violation. What happens if this secure bond is violated in a way that a spouse is left alone when he or she is most helpless and desperate? The violation is experienced as a betrayal of trust or abandonment at a crucial moment of need. An injury has been inflicted. It is a wound to their marital bond.

These times of crisis are different for different people. It could be a time of financial ruin, job loss, physical danger, physical illness, birth, death, or miscarriage. The worst example however is infidelity. Instead of being a safe haven for comfort, the offending spouse becomes a source of fear and danger.

"You weren't there for me. You left me alone. My hurt didn't matter to you. You didn't care. Never again will you do that to me."

Educational Psychologist Susan Johnson of Ottawa, Canada, published a book, *Emotionally Focused Couple Therapy with Trauma Survivors,* which deals with this problem. She says the abandonment or betrayal is seen as a defining moment in the lack of dependability of the offending partner. Tragically, at a time of great vulnerability and when presence and comfort was most essential, their partner was missing in action - or in the case of an affair or money fraud, the one delivering blows instead of comfort.

In some cases, this last traumatic episode becomes the symbolic loss of trust that accumulated because of a repeated history of similar letdowns.

No resolution. If apologies or reassurances are given, they aren't good enough or they are not believed. The injured spouse can't let it go. The traumatic incident takes on a disproportionate influence on their relationship from that time forward. Reminders of the traumatic event trigger emotion with renewed intensity. Sometimes the wounded partner retreats into a state of being numb and shuts down.

If the offending spouse responds to the hurt by discounting, denying, dismissing or simply not "getting it", it is a double wound. This intense defensive reaction is provocative to the injured partner. Repeated conversations about the "event" confirm the inner experience of disappointment and hopelessness for each partner.

The offending event becomes the subject of constant bickering, hostility and a part of an inflexible attack/defend cycle of the "here we go again" variety. The aversive interactions between them cause marital partners to withdraw into despair, alienation and aching loneliness. Even if the hurtful event is not openly discussed, it is still there producing tension and emotional isolation.

Resolving relationship injuries. The antidote to violations of the security and safety of the relationship is a willingness to take a risk to confide one's inner hurt and to have it received compassionately and non-defensively.

The offending spouse needs to be strong enough to emerge from his or her state of withdrawal or defensiveness and become engaged and then stay engaged while their injured partner describes the impact of the offense and its significance.

Confiding in each other. As he or she is being truly listened to, the injured partner's anger often dissolves into feelings such as hurt, helplessness and fear. The hurt partner shares grief over the loss of connection and trust the offense caused. The offender, by really listening and understanding his or her partner's pain, starts to empathize with the harm that was caused. In demonstrating genuine empathy, the connection between them becomes reestablished.

The offending partner needs to take responsibility for the event, and acknowledge the pain and hurt he or she caused, expressing concern, sorrow, remorse and regret along with promises of the future safety of the relationship. This is followed by an expression of his or her own grief and loss in the relationship since their bond was weakened. The process of mutual confiding with emotional openness and intensity pulls each other back into the relationship.

Physical closeness. Confiding to each other needs to be accompanied by touch, affection and physically holding each other. Both partners take emotional risks in either reaching out compassionately or by asking for comfort, reassurance and caring. The caring way this is done acts as an antidote for the lack of comfort in the original incident.

It is a beautiful, special time when couples reaffirm their commitment to stand by each other again. It is like a marriage vow being said again with two broken hearts coming together, truly knowing what it now means to be loyal and trustworthy. They now have a rekindled hope that they can find comfort in the shelter of each other's arms.

WHAT MAKES A GOOD ENOUGH APOLOGY?
CHAPTER SIXTY

I read a book called the *One Minute Apology*. It had some nice thoughts about how relationships can be restored by frequent and well meant apologies.

It is true. Not enough people make apologies for the acts of harm they have caused. It is often the missing factor in holding up forgiveness. Too many harmful actions haven't been acknowledged and the victim is left dissatisfied and unresolved.

Apologies can be cheap. What bothered me about the book was its title. A "one minute apology" may be woefully inadequate for the type of offense caused. It seems cheap and easy.

People think they have apologized with a brief, "I'm sorry!" and expect that it counts. Then they wonder why the matter persists as a deep hurt that won't go away. The problem was with their apology. It wasn't long or deep enough. It didn't address what the victim needed to hear.

I wish the book were called *The Twenty Minute Apology,* to convey what it takes to restore a relationship and open the door to true forgiveness.

I shared this thought with a client. She responded, "I'd settle for a one-minute apology." Her husband, in the middle of his stubborn pride, has consistently refused to acknowledge mistakes. Even a one minute apology would bring a soothing balm to that relationship and help her transcend the misery of real life transgressions.

The good enough apology. Apologies that minimize guilt, are defensive or cast blame, inflict more pain. Poor apologies show a lack of understanding, a lack of respect and a vulnerability that the offense could happen again. A good apology is a key to restoring the vital connection for couples - that they can be a safe haven for each other and are free again to be vulnerable and intimate.

In her book, *How Can I Forgive You?*, psychologist Janis Abrams Spring discusses the various elements of a good apology.

1. Take personal responsibility for the pain and hurt you have caused.

2. Make your apology personal. Show that the apology is about the other person and not about yourself.

3. Make your apology specific. Describe in detail the offending actions and how it harmed the other party and the relationship. This is where the apology can stretch out.

4. Make your apology deep. Be honest and truthful. Go deep into yourself and explain your motives, lapses in judgment and shortcomings, however painful or embarrassing it might be.

5. Make your apology heartfelt. Convey a transformation of the heart through body language, tone of voice, and expressions of genuine remorse. Strip away any pride and defensiveness.

6. Make your apology clean. You can't accuse someone and apologize at the same time. Don't try to explain your offense based on the other party's actions. This is not the time. He or she may or may not acknowledge their role at another time. This is not the time to assign blame. An apology is about feelings, not facts.

7. Apologize repeatedly. For serious emotional wounds, one apology may not be enough. Don't be sorry. Be sorrowful - and continue to be sorrowful as long as necessary. Don't be angry or put time limits on another's grieving. Be patient to allow your spouse time to work through the process at his or her pace.

8. Make a specific commitment not to re-offend. The commitment at the end of an apology is an anchor for rebuilding trust in the relationship. Take this seriously. Any misstep or repetition of the offending behavior after a truly meaningful apology could be fatal.

9. Make whatever amends are possible. Show a constancy of love and concern that becomes habitual and dependable.

When these steps are skipped or taken lightly, the process of reconciliation is much more difficult for the hurt party.

The miracle of apologies. I have seen the miracle of apologies unlock a frozen heart and heal unbelievable hurt. Many times the offenders are highly motivated but lack understanding of what is required.

Sometimes I coach offenders on how to make a good apology. I model a good apology. I describe the elements that they need to cover in the apology. I encourage them to use their own words but to be thorough in their apology.

When I am privileged to witness a heartfelt apology, I feel I am witnessing something sacred. My presence doesn't matter. Neither does my coaching. What does matter is how deeply the offender feels about his or her transgression and how he or she reaches out to their partner or family member with genuine remorse and contrition.

WHAT DO YOU DO WHEN THERE IS NO APOLOGY?
CHAPTER SIXTY-ONE

What do you do when someone close to you won't apologize or does nothing to right the wrong of a grievous offense? Is your only choice to forgive or not forgive?

Cheap forgiveness. Forgiveness given too easily is likely to be forgiveness that is superficial and undeserved. It is given before the hurt party has a chance to process the impact of the violation. It doesn't ask enough of the offender and short-circuits many steps that need to occur for safety and trust to be restored.

When forgiveness is given too quickly, the hurt person lives with a self-imposed prison of hidden pain, anger or rejection that he or she can no longer legitimately discuss.

Refusing to forgive. By refusing forgiveness, the injured party wants to punish the unremorseful offender and uses their refusal as an angry and continued protest of the violation. Protesting injustice becomes more important than happiness or peace of mind. Clinging to hate may be a way of hiding from pain.

Refusing to forgive can be a futile attempt to get the offender to care. Sometimes people who refuse to forgive confuse forgiveness with compassion or reconciliation, neither of which they are prepared to offer. Withholding forgiveness gives a ready weapon in future disputes.

By not forgiving, the victim chooses to live within a self-imposed prison of anger, rage, bitterness and obsessive preoccupation with injustice. Refusing to consider any of the offender's efforts as worthy of forgiveness creates a permanent wedge between themselves and the offender. Unfortunately this untreated wound drives others away also.

Genuine forgiveness. Forgiveness comes as a transaction between the victim and the offender. The offender's actions are important in meriting forgiveness. The offender invites forgiveness by understanding and acknowledging the harm that was caused, making amends, giving heartfelt apologies, and making a commitment to not repeat the wrongful behavior.

The hurt party lets go of resentment and further retribution. Healing occurs in the context of a caring relationship. It is hard to forgive when the offender isn't available or shows no remorse.

Acceptance. In her book, *How Can I Forgive You?*, psychologist Janis Abrahms Spring outlines a middle path of acceptance between cheap forgiveness and refusing to forgive. She cites Rabbi Susan Schnur's distinction between the rigid categories of forgiving and not forgiving:

"We may partially forgive, vengefully forgive, contingently forgive, not forgive yet reconcile. We may mourn yet not forgive, achieve understanding yet only forgive certain parts of the betrayal; become indifferent, become detached."

Acceptance is a healing journey you make by yourself. Genuine forgiveness is a journey you make with the offender. Acceptance can bring healing just as forgiveness can.

Acceptance is a response that can be given unilaterally when the offender is unavailable, uncaring, unrepentant or clueless as to their culpability. Acceptance also gives the victim a healthy way of staying in a relationship and offers the offender time and an opportunity to earn genuine forgiveness.

Spring outlines the benefits of acceptance. When you accept someone...

- you honor the full sweep of your emotions. You give voice to a full appreciation of the violation. You replay the injury again and again until the whole truth sinks in. You face the pain. You feel the suffering from the losses and deprivations that came with harm or injury.

- you give up your need for revenge but continue to seek a just resolution. You are more important to yourself than the need to bring justice to the offender. Punishment doesn't bring lasting satisfaction. Finding a place where your hurt can be understood and validated does.

   - you stop obsessing about the injury and re-engage with life. Obsessive, repetitive thoughts cause distress and take away energy and focus from your life.

   - you protect yourself from further abuse. You can accept someone and still not put yourself in harm's way. Acceptance doesn't mean reconciliation with someone who is likely to harm you again. By giving acceptance instead of quick forgiveness, you allow for time to pay attention to both the offender and the full consequences of the offense.

   - you frame the offender's behavior in terms of his or her personal struggles. Don't get caught up in the mistaken assumption that you caused or deserved the wrongful behavior. The mistakes are about the offender and not about you. Understanding the offender will help you respond in ways that are less vengeful, obsessive or apologetic. Understanding the offender doesn't mean you are offering forgiveness.

   Acceptance occurs when you look at your own contribution to the injury, take a balanced perspective on what happened, and learn to look at the offender apart from the offense. The final step is to forgive yourself for any personal failings in the matter.

   The goal of acceptance is to transcend the injury, achieve inner peace, find emotional resolution, get back to your best self, and find renewed meaning and value in life. It may be the best response when the offender either doesn't care, can't apologize, or won't apologize.

   Besides being a separate response to injury, giving acceptance can also be a step in a pathway to genuine forgiveness. This enables the injured party to stay in a relationship with an offender. It allows time for the offender to grasp the gravity of the offense and to do what it takes to earn genuine forgiveness.

HOW HOLDING GRUDGES HARMS MARRIAGE
CHAPTER SIXTY-TWO

One problem couples have is the inability to work through hurts and grudges. Problems are not resolved. Pain and bitterness linger long after the offense has occurred. Instead of feeling hurt, angry or anxious, the offended spouse feels resentful.

Resentment is an emotion that generally occurs when a partner whose help was counted on and was necessary lets us down and stops us from achieving something we want. Resentment is based on an assumption that our marital partner is obligated to help and that we deserved to be helped. An important goal or need was blocked or hindered by the person who we counted on the most to care and help.

When our spouse fails us, we feel hurt, betrayed and confused. Rather than question our entitlement of our goal or need, it is easier to blame our partner for his or her failure to be there to fulfill an essential obligation.

In obsessing over the mistake, a resentful spouse builds a case that the offense was inexcusable. It is easier to devalue the offender than to accept the loss and face the failure or hurt. It softens the hurt somewhat to focus on our partner's failure than to explore the meaning of the failure itself.

Trust is broken. Walls are put up. Without a meaningful apology, we stop believing that our partner really cares about us.

Anger versus resentment. Stewart Sadowsky, a clinical psychologist in private practice, Pittsburg, PA, offers these thoughts about the difference between anger and resentment.

Resentment is different from anger in the fact that anger involves an attempt to open a dialogue and a return to cooperation. Expressing anger is an attempt at communicating that change has to occur. However, a resentful spouse is not really interested in communication. If resentment is expressed, it comes out in hurtful or cutting remarks to "get even" and retaliate, not reconcile.

Anger is more related to assertiveness and moral outrage. Resentment is closer to feelings like envy, vengefulness, hatred and spite.

Anger is temporary. We think anger should "pass." We "count to ten." We "cool down." With resentment, the terminology is a little different. We "harbor" a resentment. Resentments "smolder" and "return with a vengeance." Actually, the word resentment from the French "re-sentir," which means literally, "to feel again."

Bad experiences. Outside of marriage, people carry resentments over things like a bitter divorce, a heated custody battle, a business deal gone awry, termination from employment, being an accident or crime victim, betrayal by a best friend. It might be an adult child judging past parental deficiencies. Dependent or self-centered people are especially vulnerable.

Often a person assumes the existence of an unspoken contract between themselves and another person. The other person may not even know he or she was expected to help.

A resentful person doesn't want to hear explanations that might excuse or soften the offense. He or she is rigid to the point of not wanting to hear the other side of the story. There is a huge emotional investment in his or her perception of reality.

Grudges in marriage. Within marriage, resentments come about at times when a marriage partner is left alone during a time of threat or harm and not cared about. Grudges surface when repeated requests are ignored. When destructive habits persist, the offended spouse feels betrayed. They feel hurt when they see their spouse doing things that they feel a loving spouse should "never" do. The foundation of the bond or connection is undermined by the violation of trust.

Resentment grows when attempts to address the issue are repeatedly rebuffed or when issues are not addressed in the first place.

Nourishing resentments. A resentful person actively seeks out allies to solicit agreement about what a terrible wrong has been inflicted. He or she returns to the transgression as the central meaning of what happened. Finding people to agree with them affirms his or her self-righteous stance in the matter.

People who harbor grudges "demonize" the offender. They are relentless in seeking out others with whom they can discuss the situation. They seem compelled to do so. As time passes, the negative characterizations of the offender become more extravagant and extreme.

Occasionally they may retaliate with remarks designed to punish and inflict guilt. Unlike anger, speaking one's resentment doesn't resolve the emotion or lessen the hurt.

Most resentful people alternate between seeking out sympathetic listeners and avoiding the offender or reminders of the hurtful event. They even try to block their thoughts about it. They may be successful in curbing their resentful feelings for a time. When a reminder occurs, they experience the intense feelings they had when the offense originally occurred.

Letting go of resentment. The resentful spouse needs to express him or herself in an unfettered way. It is important for the offending spouse to listen, understand and show appropriate empathy for the harm that was done.

The talk should focus on the hurt party's understanding of the event itself, their feelings of being entitled to a different, more loving response than the hurtful one at the time.

The offending spouse can address the issue, showing a deep understanding of his or her role in the hurt, apologize, commit to making amends and "being there" in the future. The sincerity and emotional expression of the offending spouse offers an avenue of hope that the past will not be repeated. The old, rigid and judgmental perceptions are broken down and are replaced by hope that the future can and will be different.

Forgiveness becomes possible.

WHAT DOES IT MEAN TO FORGIVE?
CHAPTER SIXTY-THREE

People often get stuck with bad feelings and need help to forgive. They have to let go of their anger or hurt. Until they do, they hold back and their relationships can't grow and flourish. Sometimes a lack of forgiveness becomes a greater problem than the original offense.

Psychologist Michele Killough Nelson of Virginia Commonwealth University has researched the process of forgiveness. She has broken forgiveness down into seven stages:

1. Recognition - a belief that an offense has occurred. Recognition doesn't always happen immediately. Sometimes it occurs only after a person has reflected on what happened or after they have worked through their denial.

2. Response - the experience of at least one intense, negative emotion such as anger, hurt, shame, etc. What emotion a person experiences varies with their usual response style and the nature of the offense.

3. Re-evaluate - re-evaluation of the offense and the relationship with the offender. To keep the relationship, the offended party looks for explanations such as mitigating circumstances, excuses, and their own role in the process and tries to recall past happy memories.

4. Reframing - redefining the event. Whatever positive feelings were generated during the evaluation phase are contrasted with the bad feelings. To resolve this conflict, the person now tries to change the way he or she views the offense and the offender. By changing their beliefs about what happened or about the offender, the person reduces the intensity of their bad feelings.

5. Reduction - a reduction of bad feelings about the offense and toward the offender. There is some ill will, but the person tries to set aside some or most of the negative feelings to re-establish the relationship.

6. Restoration - at least a partial restoration of the relationship. The primary purpose of forgiveness is to restore the relationship. At this point the relationship may be renegotiated and apologies and/or restitution required.

7. Release - all bad feelings surrounding the offense have dissipated. The relationship is fully restored and can grow to new levels. This means valuing and trusting the offender enough to risk being hurt again.

Four different kinds of forgiveness. Nelson further believes that two key parts of forgiveness are reduction of bad feelings and a desire to maintain or restore the relationship. Combinations of these two factors result in different kinds of forgiveness.

1. Detached forgiveness. The bad feelings are gone and there is no reaffirming of the relationship. People forgive in this way when they realize their negative emotions are sapping their own energy and preventing them from moving on to more positive pursuits.

This is self-protective. People forgive in this way when the offender has not apologized or made restitution, when the original relationship was not close or when they believe the offender cannot be trusted.

2. Limited Forgiveness. Both positive and negative feelings exist toward the offender. Forgiveness is limited because it interferes with the growth and intimacy of the relationship. The person is careful, cautious and looks at things differently since the offense occurred.

During times of stress, bad feelings about the past surface. Limited forgiveness happens when a person is unsure about the offender's actual ability to change or when the offense has profoundly disrupted the relationship.

It is appropriate to remain angry or hurt; especially when the offender is unlikely to change. Bad feelings are reminders to be careful.

3. Quasi-forgiveness. Forgiveness is out of a sense of guilt, duty or low-self-esteem. The relationship is partially restored even though the intensity of the bad feelings remains. This happens when the offender is in a position of power over the person offended. Resentments also persist when forgiveness is granted too quickly without the offender having done his or her part to earn forgiveness.

4. Full forgiveness. There is a total absence of ill will and a full restoration of the relationship. This type of forgiveness occurs when the emotional investment is valued and the relationship is allowed to move forward unrestrained.

There is a willingness to be vulnerable and trust that the other person will not exploit this vulnerability. The offender has to be repentant and has proven by their subsequent action that he or she is now reliable. This takes time, depending on the gravity of the offense. To completely restore the relationship, trust also becomes a factor. Trust won't occur until the offender has done their part to show that true change has occurred.

TO FORGIVE IS A CHOICE, TRUST IS NOT
CHAPTER SIXTY-FOUR

L ove is a choice. Anger is a choice. To forgive is a choice. How could all these strong emotions be a matter of choice? They are choices because we have the power to decide our emotions by our thoughts, commitments and actions. Otherwise we would be passive victims of fate - of events and forces outside of our control.

We are not passive victims, but actors in shaping our own destiny. It isn't what has happened to us that matters; it is our reaction to those events that matter. It is through our ability to choose that we exercise control - we decide what things mean and how we are going to act or react.

Choosing to forgive. Victor Frankl, as a concentration camp survivor of Nazi Germany, found that the one thing the prison guards could not take from him was his ability to choose how he would respond to the depravity and inhumanity around him. No one could put chains around his attitude. It is this ability to choose our reactions, even in the most dire of circumstances, that is noble and liberating about humankind.

"Forgiveness is the most necessary and proper work of every man; for, though when I do not a just thing, or a charitable, or a wise, another man may do it for me, yet no man can forgive my enemy but myself." - George Herbert

In *Les Miserables* by Victor Hugo, Jean Valjean is transformed from being a bitter victim of injustice to a loving, giving, forgiving human being by a priest who forgave him for his act of treachery and betrayal. The act of being forgiven by someone who had every right to ask for justice placed Jean Valjean into a state of moral indebtedness - of needing to do likewise to his fellow travelers in life. The priest's act of loving forgiveness multiplied itself many times.

"He that cannot forgive others, breaks the bridge over which he himself must pass if he would ever reach heaven; for everyone has the need to be forgiven." - George Herbert

The ability to forgive is aided considerably by the offender's recognition of the harm done, heartfelt remorse, an explicit apology, restitution where possible and/or a commitment not to repeat the offense. Too often, matters are left unresolved because the offender hasn't sought or asked for forgiveness.

"It is easier for the generous to forgive, than for the offender to ask forgiveness." -E. Thomson

The difference between trust and forgiveness. Some people may feel they can't forgive until they can trust again. Trust has to be earned. Trust takes time. It takes experiencing the consistency of the change. It means truly believing that the offending act will never happen again.

People don't have to wait until they fully trust someone in order to forgive them. They can forgive but if the offending act happens again, the past resurfaces as a current problem. There is something new to forgive and the journey of trust begins again along an even longer path.

Apologies are important. For some hurts, there is no restitution possible. The harm is irrevocable. The most healing action possible may be an expression of true remorse and responsibility.

Past hurts still plague the relationship because there was never an adequate apology given. A sincere apology takes the burden of responsibility from the offender and puts the matter in the hands of the offended. A few humble words may be all that are necessary to help the victim let go of the hurt.

So, what if an apology isn't forthcoming? The road to forgiveness is harder but still must be traveled. To hold onto harm is to suffer unnecessary pain. We have to forgive anyway, for our own sake. Justice is turned over to God, the ultimate Judge, while we free ourselves of the pain of waiting for justice to happen.

"Never does the human soul appear so strong and noble as when it forgoes revenge, and dares to forgive an injury." - E. H. Chapin

It is easier to forgive than to trust. We can forgive unilaterally and unconditionally. Trust depends on the actions of another. Forgiveness is given; trust is earned. Scripture requires us to love and forgive our enemies, not to trust them. Forgiving means letting go of anger and hurt. It doesn't mean exposing ourselves further to hurt. That also is a choice.

To restore a relationship to its full potential, a commitment to change needs to be followed by genuine changes. This will open the heart to risk trust again. The changes have to be real and sustained. The offending action must not occur again. Once a person has confidence that the offending act will not occur again, then trust will begin to blossom.

Not trusting doesn't mean you haven't forgiven the offense. It means more situations need to occur before trust is earned. For the offender, there is a price to pay to restore trust. Trust is restored by consistent demonstration over time that the change is real and permanent.

A history of false steps - of broken promises and repeated offenses - makes trust harder to achieve. The offender needs to be patient and to understand that their good intentions are not enough. Restoring trust takes time.

How often do we forgive? As often as necessary. How long does it take to trust again? As long as necessary.

Part XII: Making Your Marriage a Delight

When people are truly in love, they experience far more than just a mutual need for each other's company and consolation. In their relation with one another they become different people... They are made over into new beings.
- Thomas Merton

YOUR BANQUET FOR LIFE

CHAPTER SIXTY-FIVE

Your banquet has several courses. Each course is an important part of the meal. It takes practice to do it right. You need the best ingredients. The service is exquisite. The table is set with love, beauty and order.

Ingredients: a man and a woman – each strong, each courageous, each honest, each a well defined, independent personality, each with their own lofty goals and aspirations. You are matched intellectually, emotionally and spiritually. The selection of ingredients is a most serious enterprise. The success of the banquet depends on the initial chemistry of well-chosen ingredients.

The Appetizer: Attraction. Sexual attraction is a part of your journey of mutual discovery. Then comes fun, easy conversation, humor, friendship, shared values and common interests. Those exhilarating days of the first bloom of love are heady indeed. But there is so much more to follow.

Memories of the attraction are reminders that the initial chemistry was good. This admiration, respect and awe of each other's qualities are the building blocks of your love. This is the magic that brings you together.

Love evolves as you each grow in awe of the other's gifts, talents, and qualities. Admiration and respect melt the heart and create the anticipation of something even better and more wonderful to follow.

First course: Commitment. Affection is not given freely until hearts have been won and commitments made. This banquet can only be served in all its magnificence when full commitment is given. Anything less will seem like fast food.

Commitment means being loyal and faithful to your loved one. There are parts of your life that will only be shared with your loved one. Care is taken to prevent other loyalties or affections from taking your loved one from his or her rightful place in your heart.

You each are willing to pay the price to forsake all others and be committed solely and exclusively to each other. There is confidence in your choice and you each cement that choice with a covenant to be faithful under all circumstances.

Your love won't unfold and grow without confidence and vulnerability. This is a time that you take risks, share thoughts and feelings, expose weaknesses, negotiate differences and forgive mistakes.

You will become closer when there is safety for growth and change, for honesty and individuality. You rely on your commitment to provide the opportunity to explore the full range of your differences. This takes trust, which in turn, makes love greater.

Your loved one is a genuine friend - someone who respects confidences, believes the best, shows patience, gives encouragement and stays loyal when there might be reasons not to be. This takes honor.

Second course: Acceptance. Only the best of feelings will make this banquet special. Keeping hostility, criticism and negativity to a minimum maintains good feelings. A soft tone in your voice, patient listening, joyful greetings and an understanding heart show care for each other.

Out of love and respect, you choose not to retaliate or respond in kind when your loved one is out of sorts. You might be justified, but the cost to the relationship is not worth it.

You each need a friend who keeps confidences, gives another chance, and overlooks errors. You share goals and dreams. You believe and pray together. You are involved in each other's lives and know one another intimately. You share intimate thoughts and feelings, secret joys and daunting struggles. The more you share, the safer it feels.

One can be foolish, wrong, and difficult or out of sorts and still be loved. This takes vulnerability.

But you are still different – sometimes frighteningly, painfully and surprisingly so. Each has weakness. You are quick to acknowledge them and ask for forgiveness. You forgive quickly. You learn to accommodate each other. You choose not to fight when it would be easy to do so. You strive to keep out unnecessary negative conflict and criticism. You accept each other's differences and individuality. Some things will never change. Both are imperfect. You learn to live with the painful differences. This takes tolerance.

Third course: Communications. Having attraction, commitment and acceptance aren't enough. You need to communicate and solve problems together. It takes great concentration and selflessness to be a good listener. Listening is a powerful way of showing love and concern – it shows recognition that what your partner has to say is important.

You listen with your heart. You listen to understand. You suspend your own opinions, judgments, agenda, arguments and solutions so you really hear what your partner is saying. You try to understand before responding. This takes discipline.

There are times when, motivated by loving concern, confrontation is necessary. It is a step taken reluctantly with great consideration, tentativeness, and respect. The language used should be soft and gentle, yet firm and resolute.

Each of you dares to speak the truth and share the wisdom you have, even though it may not be well received. At times it is necessary to be a gentle, loving critic. This takes courage.

Problems need to be solved, differences worked out. The joys and struggles of the heart need to be shared. You listen to the soul's cry when hardship, hurt or loss crosses its path.

Main course: Love. You are the first to love for love creates love. You put your loved one ahead of yourself with daily acts of consideration, soothing encouragement, appreciation, smiles and kindness, doing it even when you are tired, out of sorts or stressed.

Love is a habit of the heart. Needs are seen, anticipated and met

– sometimes even before needs are expressed. You serve and help one another consistently and daily, making life less difficult for each other. You go the second, third or even fourth mile if you have to.

Your love shows unity as you plan and set priorities and goals for the future. You love to hear about or be involved with each other's work and activities. Family goals, children, material comforts and vacations are opportunities to come together in a special way. Your spiritual beliefs are shared and practiced.

Children and grandchildren enlarge your capacity to love. This love is not for you alone but extends outward from family to friends and strangers along the way. You invest yourselves in the relationship. This takes work.

Dessert: Romance and passion. Loving couples spend time together. You enjoy each other's company. You are playful and have fun together. This meal tastes best when it is shared. You make wonderful memories.

Your thoughtful surprises, gifts and remembrances are pleasant ways to make your loved one feel cherished and special. The extra effort is well worth the price.

Non-sexual affection, hugs and touches are freely exchanged. Great moments of sexual passion and desire occur in a context of daily love and consideration. Coming together to enjoy physical intimacy is a fitting description for the dessert in a satisfying banquet.

You enjoy the banquet. It is well worth the work and sacrifice you put into it.

CHERISHING: AN EXALTED FORM OF LOVE
CHAPTER SIXTY-SIX

C herish: to feel or show affection for, to keep or cultivate with care, to harbor in one's mind deeply, to hold dear. Even the sound of the word cherish evokes tenderness, warmth, value, sweetness. How do you know if you are in a relationship where you are being cherished?

Cherishing is selfless. To cherish, one sets aside self-interest and affirms through acts of love the value of his or her partner. Cherishing is an exalted form of love that manifests itself through thoughtful, considerate acts of kindness. Being cherished means being looked after and cared for. It is knowing that you matter, really matter. You know this by your mate's obvious concern for your happiness. You know this when you consistently experience your own well being as your partner's first concern.

Cherishing is intimate. Cherishing is the desire to connect with your loved one at a deep emotional level. You want to know your partner's intimate feelings and thoughts and are willing to share your own. You are each other's best friend. You know and like each other better than anybody else. You feel safe and secure enough to share feelings openly and honestly. Cherishing means becoming more deeply involved, more responsive, more available, and more intimate.

One cherishes by wanting to know your mate's desires and opinions, by making decisions together that affect the relationship and by planning together. Instead of living parallel lives, there is a conscious effort to coordinate and mesh your lives, to find mutually enjoyable activities, and to voluntarily become interdependent.

Cherishing is giving. Cherishing is giving the gift of the one thing you really control, the gift of to whom, and to what you bestow your attention and affection. Being generous with your resources is another way of cherishing, but not as a substitute for the personal interest and awareness you give. Cherishing requires sharing time and space together. Couples cherish each other by making a conscious effort to cultivate, renew and celebrate their relationship on a daily basis.

Cherishing can be extremely selfish if one cherishes other things above primary relationships – such as money, cars, jewelry, collections, recreational hobbies, creative work, exercise and obsessions of all kinds. Some of these things can be noble, inspiring, beautiful and worthy of great affection. They have their place in a balanced life but not at the expense of neglecting what really matters.

It is hard to imagine being cherished if you don't feel sought out, if your company is not enjoyed, if you are not remembered and if what you have to say and feel isn't listened to or valued. It is hard to imagine being cherished if your spouse consistently chooses other activities or pursuits without caring how they might affect you or your relationship.

Cherishing is kind. Cherishing is being there when needed - to really "get it" when your spouse is struggling or going through something hard. It is reaching out with open arms and words of sympathy and comfort. To be cherished is not being left alone with fear, threat or trauma.

To be cherished is to be treated with respect and dignity. You care enough to restrain your temper, show consideration in your requests and respect each other's ideas, opinions and gifts. Cherishing requires giving up the toughness, harshness and impatience that often comes by putting one's own agenda first. Cherishing does not demand nor does it keep score.

Cherishing is expressive. To be cherished is to be noticed for your goodness, to be appreciated for your loving actions and to be verbally reminded of your worth. Expressions of love through words, gifts, thoughtful gestures and remembrances communicate directly and powerfully how one feels about the other.

More than anything, cherishing is communicated through small, non-verbal acts of tenderness. It is shown by reaching out to hold hands, by gently giving a tender touch on the arm, back, or shoulder or by wanting to be next to each other.

Cherishing is supportive. One who cherishes regards another not as an extension of self but as a unique, special individual. To cherish is to accept one's spouse as he or she is now and to encourage and support their endeavors to achieve their highest potential.

To cherish is to give freedom and trust to your partner so that he or she can engage in pursuits that develop their talents, give enjoyment and stretch their capacity. This is done even if great sacrifices are involved.

Cherishing is forgiving. One who cherishes envelops another with a cloak of acceptance, dignity and respect. There is room for mistakes without penalty. There is room for compassion, for forbearance and for forgiveness. Mistakes, even big ones, are viewed as essential to the process of becoming. To cherish is to be quick to find a way to repair the breach if something has damaged your love or unity.

It is easy to cherish if you see in your loved one a reflection of your own humanity. Cherishing means treating your mate with the same tenderness, compassion and consideration as you yourself would like to be treated.

A QUICK CHECKLIST FOR A LOVING MARRIAGE

CHAPTER SIXTY-SEVEN

Include **God in your life.** Pray as a couple. Worship together. Serve others and give of your love freely. Live up to those principles you know to be true.

___ OK

___ Needs improvement

Have regular meals together. Don't allow reading, TV or music to interfere with that special time.

___ OK

___ Needs improvement

Give warm greetings to each other. Make your greetings half as enthusiastic as a family dog greeting a family member and you'll be OK.

___ OK

___ Needs improvement

Be light-hearted. Cultivate a sense of humor and, as a couple, be playful and make fun for yourselves. Make time for vacations and adventures.

___ OK

___ Needs improvement

Express your love and affection. Make touch, hugs, and physical intimacy a special part of your lives. You can nourish your marital bond through your willingness to meet each other's needs in this vital area of marriage.

___ OK

___ Needs improvement

Be loyal. Protect your marriage through keeping confidences and disciplining your heart for your partner and your partner only. Get professional and spiritual counseling for those problems that the two of you are unable to resolve.

___ OK

___ Needs improvement

Share your heart. Don't hold back on your private thoughts. Let your partner know the details of your life and be interested in his or her life. Talk about what is bothering you, what is good, what is great and not so great.

___ OK

___ Needs improvement

Listen with your heart. Learn to concentrate on your partner's thoughts and feelings and detach as much as you can from your own concerns and point of view. Seek to understand as well as to be understood.

___ OK

___ Needs improvement

Be the first to love. Love freely. Put your partner's well-being ahead of your own. Be there to comfort and soothe during times of trial and sorrow. Be cooperative and helpful. Make life less difficult for your partner.

___ OK

___ Needs improvement

Be courteous and considerate in the way you talk to each other. Avoid put downs, name calling, blame, sarcasm, harshness, rudeness, judgments, and self-righteousness. How you treat one another during conflict is more important than the dispute you are trying to solve.

___ OK

___ Needs improvement

Be accepting. Minimize or sidestep unnecessary conflict. Don't let your differences get in the way of your mutual enjoyment. Your positive interactions have to be disproportionately large compared to negative ones for the negativity to be absorbed into the marriage.

___ OK

___ Needs improvement

Be patient and accepting of differences - even long-suffering. Some changes take time. Some will never happen. Live with your differences.

___ OK

___ Needs improvement

Operate as a team. Accept each others' ideas and influence. Communicate and negotiate. Coordinate your lives. Make decisions together.

___ OK

___ Needs improvement

Be careful with anger. Don't try to solve problems while you are angry unless your spouse is really listening to you. Be willing to disengage quickly and not pursue an argument when either you or your mate is too upset to listen.

___ OK

___ Needs improvement

Be quick to apologize. Be quick to forgive. Be specific about what you are sorry for, make a commitment to improve and then follow through on your commitment.

___ OK

___ Needs improvement

Manage your resources wisely. Avoid debt. Live within your means. Share the work. Plan and dream together. Be united in your priorities and budgeting decisions.

___ OK

___ Needs improvement

Have children. Don't be afraid or put off too long the joy that children can bring to your life. Forming a family and raising children is a fundamental part of life and future happiness. Through parenting together, you will grow in your capacity to love.

   ___ OK

   ___ Needs improvement

FINAL THOUGHTS: WHAT I WISH COUPLES KNEW ABOUT MARRIAGE

It is important to nurture and meet the emotional needs of each other as the foundation of love. Love is the expression of attitudes and behavior in which the well-being of your spouse is first and foremost. Your happiness is not complete without your partner's happiness. This loving consideration is expressed in many ways in the constancy of daily actions. The loveliness of marriage comes with daily doses of kindness, consideration, courtesy, thoughtfulness, affection and appreciation.

- **It is important for couples to share the emotions, struggles and triumphs of daily life with each other.** Too many couples grow apart by not talking enough. Without mutual goals and a shared lifestyle, the marital bond weakens and suffers when life gets too busy or too hard. Don't internalize problems and withdraw emotionally. To share difficulties is to invite care and new ideas into your life. Listen to your loved one's struggles as well.

- **It is important to take the time to really listen and understand each other before reflexively giving one's own opinion.** Listening seems to be a lost art. Poor listening leads to misunderstandings and poor relationships. Too many couples don't listen well. Relationships skills can be learned.

- **It is important to talk out problems instead of ignoring or avoiding them.** Problems can be solved through communications and respectful dialogue. Too many avoid conflict and allow anger and resentments to grow while problems remain unresolved.

- **Anger and temper problems are destructive in relationships and need to be nipped in the bud through disengagement, self-control and patience.** Frustrations can be expressed in more thoughtful ways. Too many couples haven't learned to control their tempers and damage their relationships through angry outbursts. It is important to eliminate destructive behaviors that are incompatible with loving relationships.

- **It is important to learn to manage personal stress rather than have personal stress and workplace frustrations spill over on to each other.** Too many couples are unaware of how their negative emotions and poor emotional control affect people around them.

- **Couples need to be mutually supportive and involved with each other's lives.** Work is an important part of successful living. Be supportive when the additional pressures of the home and work add complexity and stress to life. Too many couples allow the stress of their work and family responsibilities to come between them. They don't learn to work together and cooperate as a team.

- **It is important to seek help for marital difficulties before problems become magnified and too much damage has been done.** Too many men don't take their wives unhappiness and complaints seriously enough and don't go for help until their wife's motivation for change has been sapped and she wants out of the marriage.

- **Couples need to communicate well during crisis and adversity.** Too many spouses feel isolated, alone and helpless during times of stress when their mates refuse to communicate or when they lash out with anger and blame. What they need is care, comfort and a listening ear for each other's thoughts and feelings. Couples need to find safety and comfort in each other's hearts and arms.

- **Marriage needs an atmosphere where fun, light-hearted humor and play are a regular part of being together.** Too many couples are too involved with their work or parenting. They lose track of how they need to find a place for humor, companionship and fun in their lives.

- **It is important to live a balanced life where marriage is enhanced by positive relationships, leisure, friendships, reflection, spirituality, service to others, and deep communications.** As there is a need for togetherness in marriage, there is also a need for separateness and personal development.

- **It is important to help your spouse grow and be the kind of person he or she wants to be and is capable of becoming.** Your spouse is a person who needs to grow, to experience newness, change, self-discovery and accomplishment. Sacrifice helps make it happen. In your own efforts for growth, be open to loving criticism and caring concern.

- **It is important to keep your marriage full of romance, affection, sexual passion, and to let your loved one know he or she is desired and attractive.** Don't lose track of the special chemistry that makes this relationship different from all others.

- **Success in marriage requires dedication and commitment, in other words, hard work.** But this work is a labor of love. The payoff will be a secure, loving relationship that will be a fountain of joy and a refuge for life's sorrows. Your legacy of marriage will leave your children to joyfully embrace marriage, unafraid of its challenges and confident in their ability to succeed both in life and in love.

Order Form for *To Have And To Hold*

To order additional copies of
To Have and To Hold
please complete the following.

$14.95 EACH
(plus $3.95 shipping and handling for the first book, add $2.00 for
each additional book ordered. Bulk rates available.)

Please send me _____ book(s) at $14.95 + shipping and
handling

Methods of payment:
Bill my ___ Visa ___ MasterCard Expires____ /_____
Card # _____
Signature_____
Daytime phone number (_____)_____

I am enclosing $_____
___Check ___Money Order payable in US funds.
No cash accepted. Orders by check allow longer delivery time. Money
order and credit card orders will be shipped within 48 hours.

Send this order form to:
JV Publishing, LLC
P.O. Box 886
Casselton, ND
58012

Ship To:
Name_____
Mailing Address_____
City_____
State/ZIP_____

Additional order forms available online
www.valfarmer.com
This offer is subject to change without notice.